STEAM RAILWAYS OF THE WORLD

PATRICK WHITEHOUSE

CHANCELLOR
PRESS

Photographic acknowledgments

John Aiosa 198, 199, 224–225 top, 224–225 bottom, 226–227; P. M. Alexander 8–9, 148–149; P. C. Allen 77 bottom; Mal Austin – 707 Operations 229; P. J. Baker 228; Hugh Ballantyne 13, 17 bottom, 19, 54–55, 56–57, 72 top, 73, 74–75, 76 top, 84 top, 88, 90 bottom, 91, 94 bottom, 110–111, 112, 113, 114, 115, 116 bottom, 117, 118–119, 120–121, 122 top, 122–123 bottom, 123 top, 124 top, 124 bottom, 124–125, 128 top, 128 bottom, 129 top, 129 bottom, 148, 149 top, 150 bottom, 154, 156 top, 156 bottom, 157, 204–205, 206, 207, 208–209, 213, 215 bottom, 215–217, 236–237 bottom; George Bambery 195; R. J. Blenkinsop 20 top; J. M. Boyes 152 bottom; D. M. Brazier 184, 185 top; China Railway Publishing House 130 bottom, 130–131, 134 top, 138–139, 234–235; A. Eaton 16, 25, 26, 47, 49 bottom, 61 top, 68, 69 bottom, 72 bottom, 77 top, 83, 166, 167, 180, 183; Emerald Tourist Board 196–197; P. Girdlestone 96, 236 top, 237 top; A. V. Haymes 89, 116 top, 151, 162 top, 164 bottom, 172, 172–173, 173, 220 top; Hotham Valley Tourist Railway 200–201; P. J. Howard 78 top, 144–145, 152–153; David Ibbotson 222–223; Peter Levy 159; Millbrook House Collection 190–191; G. W. Morrison 43 top; Jim Shaughnessy 24, 185 bottom, 190; J. B. Snell 182, 202–203; South Africa Railways 82 top; Wolfgang Stephen 169; Tim Stephens 153 bottom; Neil Tate 200; John Titlow 62–63 bottom, 69 top, 126–127, 165, 168, 210–211, 212, 214, 220; Eric Treacy 158 top, 158 bottom; C. M. Whitehouse 34–35, 37 top, 84 bottom, 106, 150 top, 160–161, 162, 170–171, 174, 177, 187; P. B. Whitehouse Collection 153 top; Alan Wild 82 bottom, 232 top, 232 bottom; D. W. Winkworth 164 top, 178 bottom; Ron Ziel 70 top, 70–71 top, 186–187 bottom, 222 top; Ron Ziel/P. B. Whitehouse Collection 12 top, 179, 181.

All other photographs by P. B. Whitehouse

Frontispiece: SP140 leaving Naoabad, Sind Province, Pakistan (*Hugh Ballantyne*)

First published in 1988 by
The Hamlyn Publishing Group Limited
part of Reed International Books

This 1992 edition published by
Chancellor Press,
Michelin House,
81 Fulham Road,
London SW3 6RB

ISBN 1 85152 173 9

Printed in Hong Kong

CONTENTS

FOREWORD·AND· ACKNOWLEDGMENTS

Even today, when steam has been in solid decline for around half a century, it would need an encyclopedia to cover all aspects of its world-wide operations. Throughout the West the steam locomotive has been reviled as dirty or uneconomic, yet it has reappeared in country after country, continent after continent, as a tourist attraction. In many parts of the less developed areas of the world, steam has hung on by the skin of its teeth, defying the all-embracing clutches of powerful diesel and oil lobbies usually because it has been an essential reserve – a simple machine within the monetary and physical capabilities of its owners and their workforces. But even steam engines wear out, and lack of heavy repair facilities and the unavailability of spare parts have taken their toll. This means that the isolated pockets which drew the enthusiast in the 1970s and early 1980s will soon be without working steam engines, sad though it may be.

Fortunately the tourist steam revival has meant a resurgence of life in the West and the almost unbelievable has happened – steam locomotives can be found alive and very well indeed in Great Britain, continental Europe, America and Australasia. Other lands where the decline has only just begun use their steam power to maximum advantage; South Africa, India, Pakistan and China are prize examples. China has the last factory in the world producing new steam locomotives, to the tune of five a week.

This book does not set out to cover each and every steam railway the world over but rather to paint a picture of recent operations, glancing at a sample of today's workings, occasional and tourist; it also takes a peep into tomorrow but this can only be a peep, for in the long run main-line steam haulage has little chance of any tomorrow. Maybe we are in the middle of an Indian summer; if so, it behoves all who are interested to stir their stumps and go forth to look, for there is much to behold in spite of the Jeremiahs who might tell you otherwise.

No book of this kind can be written without a great deal of help from others or the consulting of many erudite works, both books and magazines. The problem has not been what to include but what to leave out and I am most grateful for the advice which has been given to me by so many friends, some of whom have been kind enough not only to check out facts but also to point out errors. In particular I would like to thank Phil Girdlestone, Alan Wild and David Wardale for their assistance on the possible march forward which steam could take; their practical knowledge has helped me enormously here. Hugh Ballantyne, a seasoned traveller if ever there was one, has gone through the text and made some welcome suggestions, while David Ibbotson, Mark Brazier, Anthony Lambert and my son Michael have accompanied me for tens of thousands of miles in the past decade and a half, cameras at the ready; we have had some fascinating adventures and without their company life would have been dull indeed. John Aiosa, Don Marshall and John Snell have been able to help me out with information on the current steam scenes in Australia and New Zealand, while Jim Hutzler has allowed me the use of his Cuban locomotive lists, which is much appreciated. Other help which I am glad to acknowledge has come from R. P. Weisham, K. Simpson and Peter Levy.

I have been fortunate to have been able to travel to many places in the world where railways have taken me on safaris deep into the real countryside – a form of railway exploring which has developed into a considerable love for some of the areas concerned; of all these places I think Indonesia and China have the accolade but Africa and South America have been hard to beat. In China the China Railway Publishing House, the section of the Railway Ministry dealing with all publications from timetables to technical books, have been of great assistance to me over the past decade and I would like to say thank you to them for many happy times in that country.

I would like to acknowledge the debt which I owe to the *Continental Railway Journal*, quarterly magazine of the Continental Railway Circle, so ably edited by Lance King and his team. In its pages one can find the month-to-month goings on of steam round the world set out accurately and in easily assimilable form. Other railway journals provide news and comments, and I would like to pass on my thanks to these too: *The Railway Magazine, Steam Railway, Railway World, Colorado Annual, Trains & Railways, Baldwin Locomotive Magazine, Locomotive & Railway Preservation*; while the *Steam Passenger Service Directory*, that Bible of U.S.A steam operations, has proved invaluable. I have also looked through and refreshed my mind from various publications by the redoubtable Bill Alborough, who is the TEFS originator – the first Westerner to visit China for railways and who has now dug himself into North Korea and Vietnam. Then there are the photographers. No one, however well travelled or however expert, can have all the best pictures, so I have asked for help from those whose standard of photography is a world byword and this has done wonders to make the book really live – to these friends go my best thanks; their pictures are acknowledged in the appropriate place. It may be that I have inadvertently failed to make a personal acknowledgment; if so, I trust I will be forgiven. So much help has been given to me over the years that an exact record of those concerned would fill a volume of its own.

Last I would like to thank Jennifer Feller of The Hamlyn Publishing Group whose idea this was, and my friend and colleague Ann Wilson who has so aptly edited the typescript, not always an easy task.

PATRICK WHITEHOUSE
January 1988

CHAPTER 1

YESTERDAY'S STEAM

Preceding page: Two Castles at speed. The *Merchant Venturer*, one of the daily expresses between London and Bristol, near Chippenham in 1960. The train is a heavy one and is double-headed by two Castle class 4-6-0s. This was an Indian summer with the BR Regions having some leeway in their choice of liveries – the Western Region has reverted to GWR colours.

Born over 150 years ago and now an anachronism, the steam locomotive still thrills people of all ages, be they schoolboys, business executives, musicians, elderly clergymen, university professors or families simply seeking a tourist attraction. Even in an age of computerization, jet air travel and modern motorways, the steam railway has a magic which it potently distils. Who can resist pausing by the wayside to see a steam train pass along its steel-set way and not thrill to that pennant of steam and smoke, the roar of exhaust beats and the measured timeless stride of connecting rods? Sadly, in the Western world this is a rare sight except on tourist lines or during the occasional run of a beautifully restored veteran on main-line tracks, for in

terms of rated efficiency the steam engine performs badly. Nowadays the easy to start, ever-ready diesel or electric locomotive wins hands down even though its initial construction cost is high. Steam is labour-intensive and in modern times that will never do.

The decline of the steam locomotive is nothing new; it began seriously more than 50 years ago, particularly in the U.S.A. where there was then an abundant supply of cheap oil. The Second World War brought a temporary halt to diesel progress on the railroads with attention diverted to other essentials but, once industrial enterprise was more geared to peaceful times, manufacturers, along with the oil lobby, saw their opportunities and took them. The aftermath of war

provided many opportunities, with railway systems in Europe devastated or at the best severely worn. The scene was set when, added to this, the new post-colonial countries were hungry for outside help, particularly with new and easy to operate machines. An example of the roll-on effect of this fast-moving programme of Western dieselization became vividly apparent when, at the end of the 1960s, traffic needs on the Benguela Railway in Angola dictated the acquisition of additional motive power. An extremely efficient company, this railway relied for its prime movers on Garratts built in Manchester by Beyer Peacock, but the latter were no longer in the business, their erstwhile customers having now converted to diesel power.

Japan was the only country willing to construct new Garratts, but only at a price, so the ever ebullient salesmen from the New World made their trading ploys for diesel electrics and were successful – at least they could offer service agreements and spares, and the net began to close. Today in Angola, torn by internal strife, the diesels lie idle, too complicated for their new owners and with little chance of obtaining replacement parts. At the other end of the scale, famine relief in Uganda and Sudan has been helped by the revitalization of steam power for use on branch lines into the poorly developed areas where road access is impossible in the rainy season. But that is a story for later.

Any picture needs perspective; thus a look at the steam scene today first needs a glimpse into the past, maybe a ride on the great transcontinentals of Canada and the U.S.A. to hear the train blow in the night; a visit to the great termini of London with steam heading the Flying Scotsman, Royal Scot, Atlantic Coast Express or Cornish Riviera Limited; or perhaps a seat in the Wagons Lits diner of the Golden Arrow out of Calais, listening to the minuscule shriek of the whistle of the efficient Chapelon 231E Pacific *en route* to Paris. Other more distant but equally evocative memories include a

A heavy freight passes through the capital of Angola, then called Nova Lisboa, in August 1973: this is a long train with a banker cut into the middle. One of the tragedies of current African politics is the strife in Angola, once Portuguese West Africa. From Lobito the Benguela Railway carried passengers and freight eastwards to the Congo, down through Rhodesia and into South Africa, with a returning traffic from Zambia and the Congo in the form of copper. The railway used wood-burning British-built Garratts for its main motive power, planting legions of eucalyptus trees alongside its tracks to provide an economic fuel.

Left: The one-time Midland Railway section of Birmingham New Street station in the late 1950s showing the original overall roof. The engine is a Horwich-built Hughes-designed 2-6-0 built in the early days of the LMS; it has just brought in a local train and the calling on arm of the bracket signal is in the 'off' position, allowing a light engine to work out of the platform, probably to Saltley shed.

South Africa Railways' Garratt climbing up from George on the lovely Garden Route from Cape Town to Port Elizabeth, or sitting enthralled in an American-style clerestory coach behind a British-built Andes class 2-8-0 as it stormed up the Central of Peru towards the highest railway summit in the world. It is steam which has kept these dreams alive, the same steam which powered the pioneer railways, saw them through their teething years and into their final days of glory some 50 years ago. It was the convenience of the motor road and the coming of the aeroplane which brought rail traffic to its knees in many parts of the modern world. The diesel locomotive introduced to try to save the day has, to a degree, been the palliative rather than the cure – it came too late.

Steam also nurtured the little lines, those built into the country areas to open them up and join villages to the nearest market town. Trains were often mixed wagons trailing behind the coaches and they stopped at every crossing, loop and halt. These railways frequently were (and in some cases still are) the only real link with an outside world. Steam took both passengers and goods from the river valleys into the hills, linked hamlets and villages, and carried ore – gold, silver, copper,

Above: Pacific No. 251, unkempt and shortly to come out of service, shunts at Sennar Junction in the Sudan on 19 January 1976.

Right: Chemins de Fer du Vivarais Winterthur-built 0-6-6-0 Mallet tank No. 403 close to Le Cheyard just before closure in the summer of 1968. With a section from Tournon to Lamastre now reopened, this is one of France's premier tourist railways. In 1968 it was certainly the finest metre-gauge line in the south, whose freight was 100 per cent steam.

A pair of ex-German 2-10-0s, Nos. 56524 and 56522, climb up towards the tunnel at Gunekoy with the daily mixed train to Afyon on 26 September 1985. Both engines are fitted with snow ploughs as this hilly section can become snow-covered even in late autumn.

lead and iron – as well as countless livestock to transhipment points on the main line. Some of the railways were built to the country's standard gauge but others could not afford this luxury and were constructed on a shoe-string to narrower gauges; some were even roadside tramways running along the unpaved tracks that served as roads around the turn of the century. The varieties were almost infinite: gauges ran from standard down to 2 ft, though those in Europe were measured in millimetres. Engines came from makers throughout the Western world: Great Britain, Belgium, France, Germany, Holland and the U.S.A., with Austria's influence very much in evidence in the Balkan countries.

There was a time when you could board a sunrise local of side-door,

slatted-seat six-wheelers at the brightly painted station of St. Etienne-Chateaucreux on the edge of the Haute Loire. To get there, you took the steam route that followed the river through Bourges, Saincaize and Moulins to the rather sleepy junction of St. Germain-des-Fosses, ending up at that grimy coal and steel city, where you stayed overnight in the small hotel opposite the station. The morning train was as 'local' as the express had been '*rapide*', its motive power a low-wheeled ex-PLM 4-8-4 tank and an incredibly filthy 2-8-0 pilot. Laying a pall of brown briquette smoke behind them, the two engines climbed the spiralling gradients above the town, lifting their coaches up above the pitheads and blast furnaces and up again into the green hills; at the top of the bank the

A South Africa Railways' GMA Garratt nears the head of the Montagu Pass in the Outeniqua Mountains in September 1973. The train originated at Cape Town the day before and at this point had been travelling for over 20 hours. This is the Garden Route to Port Elizabeth where Garratts were in constant use for over 50 years.

2-8-0 came off and the 2-4-2TC ground its way alone over the twisting single track for about an hour before giving up the struggle at a tiny town called Dunieres. For standard-gauge passengers this was the end of the line but in reality it was only the beginning – for here lay one terminus of a three-legged metre-gauge network covering 160 kilometres, the Reseau du Vivarais.

Decently concealed in the luxuriant grass was a single line of casual metre-gauge track, on it an 0-6-6-0 Mallet tank with low-pitched boiler, long side tanks, shapely domes and a chimney whose characteristic flared profile claimed its builder as the Schweizerische Lokomotiv-und-Maschinenfabrik of Winterthur, Switzerland.

There was no nonsense here about starting from the platform. The narrow-gauge train headed straight out from the yard, soon settling down to a steady 25 km/h and stopping at seemingly unsuitable halts where brown-faced, dark-eyed women with loaded baskets and live hens appeared out of ditches. Along the carriage floor lay boxes of farm produce and unwilling livestock, and flapping things in sacks slid about your feet. Countless arguments about the fare took place with the conductor as the Mallet ground its way round sharp bends and along hilly ledges. Clacketty, clacketty, clacketty went the coach wheels,

cough, cough, cough the passengers, the briquette smoke drifting on to them as the entourage ran downhill. Soon the little market train was full to capacity and an hour later the Mallet wheezed to a stop at Tence. The crowd poured out, a gesticulating mass of blue, brown and black. In a second the engine was uncoupled and put into a siding, and the crew were off to the nearest café quite insensible to the scenery of stall-holders, cattle, pigs, men, women and children – it was all very, very French.

In total contrast was a ride behind steam over South Africa Railways' Garden Route between Cape Town and Port Elizabeth, a ride still of course possible behind diesel power. The journey of some 400 miles took two nights and a day. The train, a rake of clerestory-roofed coaches, left Cape Town in the early evening behind electric power – the electrification from Cape Town to Touws River was completed as early as 1954 – changing to Garratt-hauled steam at Worcester during the hours of darkness. Steam was glimpsed outside the shed at Paarden Eiland, where trip working class 24 2-8-4s shimmered in the early evening sun and old 4-6-0s lurked in sidings too far away to spot their numbers. At Worcester, late into the evening, the GMA Garratt came on, running cab first because of the tunnels on the hilly sections to come. Mossel Bay was reached just on breakfast time, with eggs and bacon served in the dining car, where spotless white cloths covered the tables, with napkins just as white lying alongside the gleaming silver, marked 'South Africa Railways', and the sparkling glasses etched with the 'SAR' crest.

At lunchtime 150-year-old George was reached, where the ritual of grate cleaning, coal trimming and watering was performed before the steep climb began up towards the beautiful Montagu Pass. This was the time to transfer to the cab for the steady ascent, as the train twisted round the sides of the green hills. Relative to any British cab, that on the Garratt was huge, almost like a bandstand with the driver as conductor. Everything was spotless: cab floor, pipework, valve handles and the driver's open-necked shirt. The more we climbed the wilder the country became, with the coastal plateau and the old town of George left far below, until the final push over the summit was made just as tea was served in the diner, 15 twisting miles and 516 m (1,693 ft) above George. It was down then to Oudtshoorn, with its ostrich farms, wide river valley and a loco shed where the Garratt came off to be replaced by a standard 19D class 4-8-2 with silvered boiler bands and all brasswork gleaming, and a huge Vanderbilt tender for the long run up to Klipplaat.

A 19D class 4-8-2, maid of all work for most branch lines still using steam, works hard on the gradient out of Alicedale with the midday mixed to Grahamstown in July 1986. The 19D class has been one of SAR's most useful locomotives, capable not only of this type of operation but also passenger trains on major services such as Oodtshoorn to Port Elizabeth on the Garden Route in steam days.

Riding on this engine in the dusk of the day up the steepening, narrowing valley into what is known as the Little Karoo was even more exciting than on the Garratt. Ahead there was nothing but the hills lit up by the setting sun and behind was the snake-like train, its carriage lights beginning to come on and the sun reflected in the glass windows. We had left a land of green fields with strutting ostriches to climb into a world of vermilion cliffs, a sight that only a poet could find the right words to describe. In their book *The Great Steam Trek*, one of the finest illustrated volumes on South Africa Railways ever produced, the authors quote Kipling's poem 'The Little Karoo' to complete a word picture of that climb up into the brown hills:

Sudden the desert changes,
The red glare softens and clings,
Till the aching Oudtshoorn ranges,
Stand up like the thrones of Kings.

Royal the pageant closes,
Lit by the last of the sun –
Opal and ash-of-roses,
Cinnamon, umber and dun.

We hear the Hottentot herders,
As the sheep click past to the fold,
And the crick of the restless girders,
As the steel contracts in the cold.

Voices of jackals calling,
And, loud in the hush between,

A morsel of dry earth falling,
From the flanks of the scarred ravine.

And the solemn firmament marches,
And the hosts of heaven rise,
Framed through the iron arches,
Banded and barred by the ties.

Till we feel the far track humming,
And we see her headlight plain,
And we gather and wait her coming –
The wonderful northbound train.

Once more in the bedroll for the night, followed by an early breakfast, and then we were in Port Elizabeth, the home of more exotic steam – the 2 ft gauge route of the Apple Express. Here were narrow-gauge Garratts and ex-German 2-8-2s built for the desert wilderness of a once German South-West Africa – new and exciting finds for the enthusiast.

Moving across the globe, memories of railways in South-East Asia teem with fascination. The Dutch in Java and Sumatra revelled in all the things impossible to perform in their small, flat homeland: they built fast lines over long distances, with mountain grades and tunnels, spindly trestles and racks, often in densely populated country; and running over the zigzags and horseshoes was a wonderful mixture of compound Pacifics, Mallets and 12-coupled tanks. The whole was un-questionably the finest 3 ft 6 in gauge

Above: A South Africa Railways' GMAM class Garratt climbs out of Graaf-Reinet with a morning freight in the spring of 1977, a long haul through arid countryside necessitating a bogie water-carrier next to the engine. Until 1976 this route was home to Graaf-Reinet and Rosmead class 19B 4-8-2s with the occasional class 24 2-8-4 or 19D 4-8-2. The whole operation is now diesel.

Left: The first-ever special train on the forestry line on the outskirts of Cepu was organized by Hugh Ballantyne on 6 August 1984. The wood-burning engine is 0-10-0 tank *Tudjubelas*, built by BMAG in 1928, one of many German machines to work in Dutch Java.

A Werkspoor 1928-built 2-6-6-0 Mallet No. 5024 brings a reminder of Dutch colonial days as it storms out of Cibatu with the midday train for Garut and Cikajang on 17 August 1979. Although the clouds of black smoke look impressive, No. 5024, like most engines in Java at the time, was not in the best condition and the train consisted of but two coaches and a van. The small boy on the left has just snagged his kite on the telephone wire.

system in the world of the 1930s and the only one which ran trains at speeds of 70 mph.

The Second World War and the political upheavals afterwards changed all that, leaving the system to run itself down to unimaginable poverty. Matters are on the mend today, though steam plays little part except to rescue failures. But images remain and you can still dream of the huge Mallets storming out of Bandung, the upland capital of Java, against a background of cone-shaped volcanic mountains. Or imagine a Krupp 2-8-2 – the classic jack of all trades in Java and an oil-burner – laying down a pall of black smoke as it pulled out of Madiun, its tubes scoured with handfuls of sand thrown

into the firebox. Above all, there was Cibatu, the last and only place in the world with a steam locomotive depot whose allocation was made up entirely of articulated types, though mostly out of service.

Cibatu was always a friendly place and any initial difficulties in communication would soon be solved by the appearance of the local schoolmaster, who would translate and answer such technical queries as to whether the Mallet tanks would be running the next day or if the shed-master could be persuaded to double-head the train for a couple of English photographers. Several times a day these huge machines trundled their way up to Garut and on to Cikajang, though the loads

yard at Surabaya's Wonokromo station, not so long ago home to a frantic service of steam trams, now swarms with families living in van bodies, old coaches and even a tram engine. New West German diesel hydraulics haunt the main lines where once Pacifics and Krupp 2-8-2s held sway, and the rack at Ambarawa lies silent. But memories remain as green as the paddy fields. In theory the local management will hire out the train but somehow the engine always needs repair.

Back in the United Kingdom there was the Indian summer of the late 1950s. Think of the footplate of a great green King heading a Birmingham to London fast – working the harder of the two roads to the capital, for the rival London & Birmingham Railway had taken the easier route via Rugby and Coventry in 1838. Based at Wolverhampton's Stafford Road shed, the Kings, though nothing uncommon and almost at the end of their lives, were tended with loving care. The 4 p.m. 'up' was a favourite train, running out of No. 12 platform at Snow Hill and stopping only at Leamington Spa. Let us recapture the joy of this ride on a King, thinking of the continuous shovelling of coal needed for the 110-mile journey – the fireman's job.

It is winter and dark when the train sets off. Dead on time a handlamp,

Smartly repainted in standard black livery, 0-4-2 rack tank No. B2503 stands raising steam outside Amberawa shed, Indonesia State Railways, on 7 August 1984. For some time the Amberawa rack section (with its museum locomotives set out in the open opposite the large island-platformed station) had operated on a tourist train only basis but lack of maintenance made even this operation spasmodic. Sadly this too was a typical railway day in Java, for B2503 became a failure on the rack some two hours later. Currently the engine is still out of service, but one never knows in Indonesia.

were scarcely those contemplated by their Dutch masters of the 1930s. Columns of black smoke rose from their squat chimneys as they left the station, at times that were rarely near the schedule, for timekeeping in Java was never the essence of exactitude. While one waited, the local children, smart in white shirts and navy blue trousers or skirts, would crowd round, full of curiosity and good humour, thoroughly enjoying themselves mimicking the Westerners.

They were happy days – all the photographer had to do was to watch that no one walked off with his camera and keep one eye open for smoke in the distance. Steam lingered on into the mid-1980s but now little moves. The

Right: The 10.00 Birmingham (Snow Hill) to London (Paddington) accelerates out of Leamington Spa behind ex-GWR 4-6-0 No. 6005 *King George I* in October 1958, ten years into nationalization. The locomotive is now fitted with a four-row superheater and double chimney, giving considerably improved performance figures.

Below: Stafford Road shed, Wolverhampton, was base for the King class ex-GWR 4-6-0 which worked the Birmingham and London expresses up until 1962. No. 6017 is being coaled at the Edwardian-type stage prior to picking up a train which will have come through from Birkenhead, Chester and Shrewsbury.

held high by the proud guard, flickers to green, a platform inspector's whistle blows and the fireman moves over to his side of the cab to slide coal through the fire-hole door. Down through the tunnel under the city centre they go, the exhaust crackling from the copper-rimmed chimney, out through suburbia and into the darkened countryside, through castled Warwick, the train a serpent gliding smoothly behind the green and gold engine; then once over the black Avon, the Leamington stop. Beyond here the running becomes harder; perhaps there is some mist too, but nothing to bother the engine crew for the Great Western Railway, alone of the four British main lines, had ATC (automatic train control) and a safety record to be proud of.

The train goes on, through the quiet of Oxfordshire, past Banbury with its shed of smoking engines and a branch into the Cotswold hills, through Princes Risborough, then over the Chilterns to High Wycombe and on to Paddington – Brunel's old terminus, its great arches still intact, and home to all

who loved the great Great Western. Fireman and engine have worked very hard; there has been no signal check nor special speed restriction and the driver has 'let her run' through the junctions, and yet they have beaten the timetable by only half a minute.

Across the sea in Ireland the mid-1950s saw the autumn of the 3 ft gauge, the largest and finest of them all the County Donegal Railway's Joint Committee. By then steam was confined to the heavier freight trains and summer specials; other passenger services ran with railcars which in fact amounted to rail-buses that stopped here, there and everywhere at the convenience of locals. Most of the line – over 100 miles of it – was still working, running from a junction with the Great Northern Railway (Ireland) at Strabane, south of Londonderry, over the green mountains to Donegal and splitting there for Killybegs and Ballyshannon, both on the wild Atlantic coast, the first a small port, the second a seaside watering hole of some popularity.

Stranorlar, County Donegal Railway's Joint Committee, Eire, in August 1957, two years before final closure. This was the hub of the system and junction for the one-time branch to Glenties. Here were the locomotive works and carriage repair depot as well as the main offices situated in the station buildings; the fine tower to the left of the church is over the gentlemen's lavatory. On the left is the remaining Baltic tank 4-6-4 *Erne* in geranium red; on the right is a late railcar No. 18 trailing a four-wheeled van (also painted red to denote that it is vacuum-braked and thus fitted for railcar duties). In the platform between is part of the stock for the August Bank Holiday excursion to Ballyshannon, painted in red and cream – the forerunner of British Railways' early 'blood and custard' livery.

No. 11, *Erne*, shunting at Killygordon between Stranorlar and Strabane in August 1959, the last year of operation for the County Donegal Railway's Joint Committee, one of Ireland's longest 3 ft 0 in gauge railways. Passenger services were run by efficient little railcars towing a trailer van for small items of goods, leaving steam to deal with the daily freight – usually one on each section.

The highlight of the steam workings were the holiday excursion runs to Ballyshannon at weekends during the summer months; one run was from Strabane and the other from Stranorlar, the hub of the system, just within the Eire border. Strabane was in the Six Counties and the meeting point with the Great Northern's 5 ft 3 in gauge line from Portadown. The trains, each hauled by one of the large geranium-red 2-6-4 tanks (all named) and using every piece of the available rolling stock, were packed to the doors, for the roads were still poor and buses few. The only booked stop *en route* was Donegal town, where a reversal was necessary to get on to the Ballyshannon branch. Here the crew took the opportunity to clean the fire and give their charges a much needed drink from the nearby water-tank.

They came back in the early evening, leaving Ballyshannon around 7 p.m., which allowed the passengers a good day out and the opportunity to return, to use the vernacular, 'a little the better for drink'. A stop at Donegal to reverse, look at the fire and water the

engine, then they were off, with the setting sun behind them. From Donegal eastwards the line ran steadily, though not yet spectacularly, towards the Blue Stack Mountains, making it wise for the crew to get to grips with the bank straight away – two shovel-fulls at the front of the firebox, pause, two at the back, pause, and so on. Once the train had cleared the crossing at Lough Eske, the real climb began and at Barnesmore Halt the 1 in 60 gradient started, with the next three miles among the most spectacular and dramatic of any Irish railway as the line clung to the slopes high over river and road.

It was now dark and looking back from the engine one could see the flashing headlights of cars as they came up the black valley, following the train throwing out great clouds of smoke which drifted back and down towards them. High along the stone embankment the train snaked and in a few moments the cars were out of sight as it passed under the Derg Bridge and made its way along the silver waters of Lough Mourne.

They were great days, those Bank Holiday excursions, and even up to the line's inevitable closure the crowds were heavy. The end came on the last day of December 1959 when the brothers McMenamin took a final freight over the West Donegal section, using the 54-year-old Baltic tank No. 14, *Erne*. They set off in the evening from Stranorlar after waiting for the last east-bound railcar and headed towards the Barnesmore Gap and the dark mountains of the west, the slow exhaust beat echoing across the quiet night into the local homes. It was a long train of supplies and coal for Ballyshannon, whose populace knew well what was to come – prices went up the following week.

Another memory, perhaps of steam at its greatest, is of the Canadian transcontinentals, where red and black Canadian Pacific or black Canadian National giants moved their huge loads from division to division. Passengers travelled behind them coach-class or Pullman, the latter with two seats by day on either side of a central gangway and upper or lower bunks by night, each shut off from the aisle by curtains.

The long heavy trains ensured that the crews would take care to stop with the buckeye couplers bunched up, giving that little extra chance when starting and pulling the train up coach by coach. Taking soup in the diner could create problems if the snatch was just that bit too hard. Equally impressive were the huge Canadian Pacific Selkirk 2-10-4s as they pounded the grades westbound from Calgary to Beavermouth, working unassisted with 12- to 14-car trains weighing between 950 and 1,100 tons, or eastbound up Field Hill with 1,200 tons.

But the greatest memory of all is of Moncton, New Brunswick, on a cold December evening in the mid-1940s, with snow thick on the ground, crisp and white, the sky clear as crystal. Moncton was a division point for the huge CNR 4-8-4s which worked the long green trains from Halifax to Montreal, and here was a shed full of steaming engines ready for locomotive changes in each direction. Standing on the platform with ear-muffs for protection from the icy wind, one watched as the change took place and a new engine, its tender already ice-

Moncton, New Brunswick, in 1943 with Canadian National Railways' 4-8-4 No. 6171 backing on to a Halifax-Montreal train. Moncton was a division point where all trains changed locomotives and hence a fascinating place for any visiting enthusiast. Contrary to much stricter conditions in the U.S.A., the Canadians were quite relaxed about railway photography at the time.

Left: On a misty morning in June 1982 one of the pretty 0-4-0 + 0-4-0 Mallet tanks, No. E163, approaches Gatao with a dawn-cracking train from Arco to Livracao, junction with the Portuguese State Railways' Douro Valley Branch. The Livracao line is the westernmost of four such metre-gauge branch lines taking trains north from the Douro Valley and the first to introduce railcars back in the early 1970s.

encrusted, was backed down to engage the buckeye couplings, its headlight shining forward into the darkness. Then down the low platform four cars to the warm Pullman sleeper to feel the jerk of the start, an ear cocked for the locomotive bell clanging for the crossing and the sharp bark of the exhaust. Lying half-asleep in the bunk bed with the curtains drawn, one listened to the eerie whoo-whoo-oo of the engine as the train made its way into unfenced territory with dozens of gateless crossings. Somehow it was the most reassuring and wonderful sound on earth. The only experience to compare with it in recent years, until the final electrification of the Trans-Siberian route, was the comings and goings of similar giant 4-8-4s in Soviet Russia.

Such are the memories of yesterday's steam. But still today, in the East and in parts of the Third World, steam not only serves but also does so as part of day-to-day operations. True, it is hard to find a prestige express that is not diesel- or electric-hauled but on secondary duties and freights steam is there in abundance. Elsewhere, when the diesel fails from lack of spares or maintenance, steam returns to run the daily, weekly, even once monthly, freight or mixed train. It survives too in such exotic places as the spice islands of Indonesia and the Philippines where sugar-cane estates use a wonderful variety of old power fed by bagasse – the baled and otherwise useless residue of cane from which the sugar has been extracted. Nor is steam dead in the eyes of people in the West, for after an initial period when its name was a dirty word, the authorities concerned with the running of the great railways of state have found that peripheral money can be made from excursions hauled by lovingly cared for steam engines,

Opposite: CNR Pacific No. 5293 at Sherbrooke, Quebec, waiting to take a night train back to Montreal on a snowy Saturday evening. The photograph epitomizes the railway scene in steam's last years and reflects the wonderful dry cold of a Canadian winter. These 4-6-2s were used on local services over most of the CNR system.

One of the last regular operations using steam in Spain was the metre-gauge line from Ponferrada to Vilabelina, running 65 km into the mountains and serving collieries *en route*. For many years this line was served by a fleet of American 2-6-2 tanks and German Engerth 2-6+4 tender tank locomotives. After dieselization of the 'main line' in 1981 much of the fleet was laid aside but examples of both types still shunt at the termini. Engerth No. 17 is seen here in October 1981, just a month before the diesels arrived, taking a drink at Cubillos after the stiff climb out of Ponferrada with a load of coal empties.

purchased by enthusiasts when all had seemed lost. A decade ago no one would have believed that Great Britain, Western Europe, Australia and the U.S.A. were the places to go for working steam on the main lines but today the wheel has turned full circle, with restored engines hard at work hauling tourists and rail fans.

No one knows how many steam locomotives are left alive in the world today but they are still numbered in their tens of thousands. New steam is being built in China; India has standardized but the old sounds still remain, as they do in Pakistan; and South Africa and Zimbabwe can still show steam, some of it very much at its best. On all five continents it is possible to hear an engine whistle. The cause is not yet lost.

A Henschel-built 2-4-6-0 Mallet tank heads a mixed train up the Corgo Valley to Vila Real and Chaves in 1969. It began its journey at Regua on the Douro Valley line, making connection with the local from Oporto, again steam-hauled – by a variety of 4-6-0 class.

CHAPTER 2

STEAM TODAY

Preceding page: En route for the Devil's Nose. A Baldwin 2-8-0 belonging to the Guayaquil & Quito Railway in Ecuador heads up through the jungle towards Sibabe and the high mountains leading to Riobamba in October 1981.

Padang port in August 1975 with a C33 class 2-6-0 tank on the daily working. These somewhat ugly ducklings – ungainly with their outside Allan valve gear – were used on the adhesion sections of the West Sumatra system both at Padang and between Batutabal and Solok.

OCCASIONAL OPERATIONS THROUGHOUT THE WORLD

The Boeing 737 from Jakarta banks and turns to make its approach into Padang airport. Through the perspex windows of the pressurized cabin passengers look down on Sumatra's silver sand running into a seemingly limitless green of paddy fields and jungle, while a muddy river makes a small estuary on the edge of the town. Close by the minuscule harbour a smudge of brown smoke drifts into the humidity of tropical Indonesia; it comes from the chimney of the only working steam locomotive in the area, the dock shunter. The plane lands and passengers disembark, the hot damp air meeting them like a wall as they descend the steps to the tarmac by the tin-roofed airport building. Outside, cars collect some returning officials while a rickety bus, cockroaches crawling on its floorboards, waits for the less fortunate.

Those who have come to seek steam may or may not be lucky, for although the dock shunter, a small 2-6-0 tank, moves spasmodically up and down its small cage-like territory, the steam-engine works is creeper-encrusted and there is only the odd fitter working more in hope than anticipation. The line into the jungle-covered hills up to Padang Panjang is officially diesel but

breakdowns are far from uncommon and trains tend to run to a peculiarly localized and unspecific timetable. So it is wise to tarry a while to make enquiries, stopping off at the only hostelry in the place that boasts any form of air-conditioning, the Mariani International Hotel. It is owned and run by a *femme formidable*, Madame Mariani, who superintends her hotel in the manner of an old-time seaside landlady, but allowing for the unavoidable insect population, the rooms are good and the toilets work; what is more the food can be extremely appetizing.

Sumatra is a very large island, mountainous and well covered with jungle; it has three separate railway systems based on Padang in the west, Medan in the east and Palembang in the south, unlinked because of the unpenetrable terrain. There was one other link, the now abandoned railway joining Pakenbaru on the river Siak in eastern Sumatra with Sawahlunto on the western system. Thousands of prisoners of war of the Japanese lost their lives building this railway during the Second World War, and the route through fever-ridden jungles and swamps must have been just as terrible as the better-known Burma–Siam Railway featured in the film *The Bridge on the River Kwai*. The weather is hot, very hot, and when it rains (which is often) the water descends in sheets. But the spasmodic appearance of steam is worth the vicissitudes, for to reach the lands beyond Padang Panjang the railway climbs the escarpment by rack using, until very recently, 100 per cent steam power in the form of Swiss, German and 1960s-built Japanese 0-10-0 tank engines. The journey takes about a couple of hours, first through the inevitable rice fields and then, once over the girder bridge spanning the tumbling river, through the evergreen of the jungle, past waterfalls, through cuttings and over gorges up to the summit. Even today the chance of steam is fair, for the depot at Padang Panjang has a large assortment of rack tanks, some very dead indeed, but some just sleeping. If the new diesel

Overleaf: Four working E10 class 0-10-0 rack tanks on the shed at Padang Panjang on 26 August 1979. On the left is E1060 built by Esslingen in 1966; the centre engine is E1016, Esslingen 1920; and that on the right E1007, SLM 1922. Most of the other engines in steam were of the later batch (as with E1060), fitted with Giesl ejectors. The whole class was extant in one form or another but the majority of engines were very dead.

Left: One of the earlier (1922/26) SLM-built class E10 0-10-0 rack tanks on the climb between Batutabal and Padang Panjang in August 1979. Despite an influx of new (1964/67) machines from Esslingen and Nippon, these Swiss engines appeared to be enjoying a fresh lease of life over this section, though the later members of their class had 100 per cent occupation on the Padang side of the hill.

Medan station yard in August 1975 with wood-burning 2-6-4 tank No. 58 and a decoupled 0-6-4 tank running as an 0-4-4 tank. The 2-6-4 tank had just arrived with a mixed train, while the 0-4-4 tank was on shunting duties. This North Sumatra system of PJKA (Indonesian State Railways) incorporated the whole of the one-time Deli Railway.

feels unwell, then one of these tanks will certainly work the train. From Padang Panjang the rack continues down the green hills and alongside paddy fields to Batutabal on the line to Solok, its nearby coal mines being the main reason for the railway's continuing existence. The rack also runs up to Bukittinggi, a popular hill resort, but the track here is so bad that this is traversed once in a blue moon and at your peril.

It is just as hot on the north-east coast, where the provincial capital of Medan also sees a small amount of steam, in the form of wood-burning 2-6-4 tanks of Dutch origin. This was the one-time Deli Railway in the coastal region of the island, facing Malaysia across the straits of Malacca; it is a land of palm trees and palm oil plantations. Steam occasionally comes to life on the section at Tebingtinggi Siantar and Kisaran, using some much more modern (but still wood-burning) 2-4-2 tanks that look something like an old Hornby train.

Less than an hour away and to the south-east lies teeming Java, a land of coned volcanoes, crowded cities, eternal paddy fields and friendly people. Sadly, little that is steam moves here today, though pockets can be found if patience is exercised – not necessarily easy in the tropical heat. Tomorrow is always an unknown quantity and is usually the day when steam is booked to work – if it had not run yesterday.

Probolingo, Bagil, Kediri (with its steam roadside tramway) and Kertosono are all possibles, as are the trains out of Madiun to Ponorogo using ancient 2-4-0s built in the last century by Sharp Stewart of Manchester. But if you are lucky, the far west of Java can still hold a trump card. Rangkasbitung lies due west of Jakarta's Tanahabang station, a shantytown city with box cars and vans standing here and there on the yard's rails, where they have obviously been marooned for years and now provide homes for countless people.

Taking the train to Rangkasbitung is a mind-broadening experience: children ride what is left of the footboards, locals crowd the roofs, the coach floors are deep in litter and the track is almost hidden among market stalls, pigs, dogs and general bric-a-brac. At the far terminus there is a shed housing 4-4-0s, some of which are still used on the branch to Labuan at the western tip of the great spice island.

Labuan is a fishing village of shanty huts and outrigger canoes, set on a small estuary, with a beach of paradise where the local hotel (the shower a tin-can pulled by a string) charges for drinking water but provides lobsters by the dozen as their cheaper meal. Just outside the village lies a single-platformed station, with a turntable which works one year and not another. It is surrounded by palm trees and overnight – on nights when the train runs – it houses the engine off the Rangkasbitung train, which comes in tender first if the turntable is not working. Literally hundreds of children hang on to all parts of the stock, their shrieks accompanying each rough shunt. The crew then go off to lodge in the station building overnight. Just on dawn at 5 a.m., B5138 of 1904 vintage, a two-cylinder compound 4-4-0, moves off into the orange-streaked sky, packed solid with the paying and unpaying, riding on the footplate and tender as well as all over the short train.

Although it is almost impossible to believe, the ancient Sharp Stewart 2-4-0s built from 1879 onwards were still at work in Java in the mid-1980s. They were kept specially at Madiun for working the roadside branch to Ponorogo and on to Slahung, a daily task hauling mixed trains. The morning train from Ponorogo is seen running behind B50.07 through the streets of Madiun en route to the junction station in August 1979. Like many other engines in Java the B50s were fitted as oil- and wood-burners. No. 50.07 was one of the two remaining members of the class left 'under repair' in 1987.

Tanahabang station in August 1975 with a train from Rangkasbitung entering behind Swiss-built class C27 4-6-4 tank No. C27.09, built in 1916. The approach to Tanahabang station is through a shanty town of disused box cars, vans and old sheets of corrugated iron on timber supports, all used as multi-family dwellings.

With the whistle shrieking for the ungated crossings, this train with its mass of humanity wends its way into the temporary cool of the morning and on towards the markets of town and city (change at Rangkasbitung for Jakarta – it is a full day's journey), forming one of the last of Java's splendidly colourful scenes of steam.

Jakarta to Kuala Lumpur is little more than an hour by jet but a much greater distance in style and politics, for the Malaysian railways are much better preserved than those in Java, though in the old days they were never in the same class. Today the metre-gauge system, one end joining with Singapore and the other with Hat Yai in Thailand, runs modern air-conditioned trains, but one or two British-built Pacifics hide away in Kuala Lumpur, kept for tourist use on the branch out to Batu Caves. The engines are cared for as well as possible, but spares are non-existent and the future is always unsure. Yet the fact that they are there at all, and far from dead, is a hopeful sign.

Until the mid-1970s Thailand was a steam mecca with magnificently kept wood-burning Japanese-built Pacifics and Mikados. Some steam was pre-served as museum pieces, including those trains at the tourist site at the River Kwai Bridge. Recently, steam as a tourist attraction has run over the branch to Ayut Thaya, usually with a 1950-built 2-8-2 and up to ten restored wooden-seated bogie coaches, though other Japanese-built 2-6-0s are often on this working. Again the climate is hot, very hot, and cold drinks – other than

water – are almost vital to Westerners beating into this edge of railway tourism.

Moving on through the East and Far East, China, as will be seen later in the book, is alive with steam, whereas Japan has none, except for occasional tourist attractions.

Pakistan and India have an abundance, the railways being the main form of transport in this vast subcontinent. Sri Lanka has little but that which moves is almost unique – a 2 ft 6 in gauge line from Colombo using very British 4-6-4 tanks and, truly wonderful, a sentinel steam railcar for special groups, running between Maradana station and Homagama, the outer terminus for steam working. The broad gauge too has some tourist steam, usually working from November to March and using either a B1 4-6-0 or a B2 4-6-0 tender tank.

Still south of, or just on, the equator and only a few hours by plane is South America, once the home of British-owned railroads. Now under national banners, these are very much in decline, some troubled simply by lack of cash, others by far more serious political problems. Steam can be found in the majority of countries in the subcontinent, but it is mostly on its last legs, except notably in Argentina.

The 05.00 train from Labuan to Rangkasbitung behind two-cylinder compound No. B51.32 (Hanomag 1904) in August 1979. This is a 3 ft 6 in gauge scaled-down example of a Prussian P4 4-4-0. The last active home shed for these engines was Rangkasbitung and their final workings the Labuan branch, though for many years they monopolized the trains to Jakarta.

Above: Maradana station, Colombo, with a 2 ft 6 in gauge train for the Kelani Valley line headed by a Hunslet-built 4-6-4 tank. This system, though truncated, still runs a quite intensive suburban service with steam in the minority but on a regular basis between the capital and Homagana, the outer terminus for steam working.

South America is a land of contrasts, one of the most decided being the Tierra del Fuego in the far south of Argentina, close to (in comparative terms) the disputed Falkland Islands. Here a 2 ft 6 in gauge railway has two plusses for the railway enthusiast: it is not only the southernmost railway in the world but it also uses steam – not just ageing relics but the largest, most powerful and very much the most advanced steam locomotives ever to run on the narrow gauge, and in the world, until the trials of the South Africa Railways 4-8-4 *Red Devil* in the early 1980s and some Chinese locomotives built at Datong even more recently. The line is the Rio Turbio and given time, cash and permission from the Argentinians, this 155-mile-long colliery railway, opened in 1951, is well worth a visit. The drawback is that southern Patagonia is bleak in the extreme – cold, windy and dusty or cold, windy and wet. Further north in Patagonia, where a form of the Welsh language is still spoken (not one necessarily understood in Wales), there are 250 miles of 2 ft 6 in gauge railway from Ingeniero Jacobacci to Esquel. This still runs steam passenger trains (usually mixed) on a regular basis. The nearest airfield is at San Carlos de Barioloche, a lake district resort in the mountain foothills.

North from Argentina and across the Rio de la Plata, Uruguay has been somewhat neglected by rail-fan groups in recent years, largely because the British-built railway there has all but abandoned steam. But steam can still be found if one searches with diligence. Down on the quayside of Monte Video a Manning Wardle 0-6-0 tank of 1888

Preceding page top: A mixed train between Ingeniero Jacobacci and El Maite in October 1981. This lonely section of railway is 100 per cent steam, using German (Henschel) and American (Baldwin) built 2-8-2s on passenger trains which run twice weekly. This is part of the General Roca Railway and has its main workshops at the small town of El Maite about halfway along the line; all trains change engines here.

Preceding page bottom: The steam depot at El Maite on the 2 ft 6 in gauge line from Ingeniero Jacobacci to Esquel in Patagonia. Visits to such places without authority were not encouraged by the Argentinians in the late 1970s and this photograph was taken in October 1977 by lucky opportunity – everyone was at lunch.

vintage comes to life on an 'as required' basis. Outside the Central Railway station – of best British lineage – the 'Railway Museum' sports an 0-6-0 tank by Black Hawthorn of 1888, an 0-6-0 saddle tank by Manning Wardle of the same period, a Hawthorn Leslie 2-8-0 of 1921 and, a sign of later nationalization, a German Henschel 2-10-0 of 1950. If you took a diesel multiple-unit out of Central station and branched north-east for two hours, you came to Sudriers. Here, lonely but well-loved, is a shapely Beyer Peacock 2-6-0 tank of 1910; another is still in steam at Florida. Further north still, some Beyer Peacock 2-6-0s work freight at Rivera, sometimes as far south as Tacuarembo. All this shows the influence that the British brought to the railways of South America in the times of expansion and prosperity, not only in Argentina and Uruguay but in the high Andes of Peru.

In Peru the great days of steam are sadly long past but even so there are some surprises in store for the observant. In the autumn of 1985 a group of enthusiasts found (and rode behind) a relic last seen statically preserved at

Lima station – Andes 2-8-0 No. 206 – the classic class once belonging to the Central Railway (FCC) of Peru, the hardest and highest route in the world. No. 206 had somehow been brought to life and was in steam at Huancayo, the Andean terminus of the FCC. It was not in the best condition, to say the least, but it still managed a special train to Jauja and back, a day's journey.

Even though the standard gauge can boast but one workable engine, there are a few locomotives just alive on the 3 ft gauge sections in the mountains out

Left: One of the more dramatic pieces of railroad in the Peruvian Andes is the 3 ft 0 in gauge line from Huancayo to Huancavelica. Once a user of Baldwin consolidations and Hunslet and Henschel 2-8-2s, this section of the Peruvian State Railway now runs diesel locomotives and railcars, though steam is kept in reserve in case of trouble. The one workable engine in 1986 was Hunslet 2-8-2 No. 107, seen here after taking water *en route* to Huancayo.

Opposite: One of the famous Andes-type 2-8-0s which once worked the principal services over the 'Highest and Hardest' from Lima to Huancayo, reaching 4,570 m (15,000 ft) *en route*; sadly, they have now been replaced by supercharged diesel electrics, bellowing out black exhaust fumes as they climb into the rarefied atmosphere. This engine, No. 206, is still lettered FCC (Central Railway of Peru) and painted in the old green livery. Originally kept for static preservation, No. 206 was steamed again in 1986 and is seen here in the high valley some two hours out of Huancayo.

of Huancayo and Cuzco. Kept only as reliefs for the new diesels or modern railcars, Hunslet and Henschel 2-8-2s still show their faces 3,050–3,350 m (10–11,000 ft) up in the high Andes. Non-Peruvian passengers are severely discouraged from riding the whole length of the railway out of Huancayo to Huancavelica, for fear of guerilla attacks. So changed has the situation become that armed guards ride the coaches of the old Central's main line, with passenger trains reduced to three days a week in each direction. At Cuzco even the shunt through the town down to the old southern station is now diesel but every once in a while one of the Henschel 2-8-2s comes to life, perhaps for a special or a works train. To see one of these blasting its way up the zigzags straight out of Cuzco is one of today's railway experiences. While it is good to know that the fabled Inca city of Machu Picchu, perched high on a mountain north-west of Cuzco, can *only* be reached by rail, steam is no longer the means.

39

The Southern Railway of Peru linked Cuzco with its southernmost capital, Arequipa, and the port of Mollendo, using a junction at Juliaca (where there are two very dead Andes 2-8-0s) for Puno on Lake Titicaca, at 3,855 m (12,650 ft) the highest navigable lake in the world. Here until very recent times, on a once weekly schedule, the splendid S.S. *Ollanta* met the Cuzco train and set sail overnight for Guaqui in Bolivia, something over 100 miles away. Though rather moth-eaten these days and used only for freight or chartered passengers, the *Ollanta* is still well kept, her gleaming brasswork a reminder of early 20th-century luxury travel; today's Titicaca sailors use a hydrofoil, but the *Ollanta* or her even older sister, the *Inca*, were the *only* links in the days before aeroplanes on the long journey from the capital of the

Left: The 3 ft 0 in gauge railway is still today's practical means of reaching the old Inca fortress of Machu Picchu from the one-time capital city of Cuzco. Steam has been officially replaced by diesel for the past five years but as at Huancayo something is kept in reserve just in case: this time two Henschel 2-8-2s at Cuzco. These engines, one of them not at all well, head a Cuzco-bound special excursion in October 1986.

Opposite top: Nemacon station in the sub-Andes with a return steam-hauled excursion to Bogota, October 1985. The engine is 4-8-0 No. 76, built by Baldwin in 1947 and designed by Dewhurst. These Sunday excursions are regular features of the 3 ft 0 in gauge Colombian Railways' operations and provide a dining-car service.

Opposite bottom: Guaqui on the Bolivian shore of Lake Titicaca in October 1985. On the left shunting the dock is Bolivian State Railway 2-10-2 No. 704 (BLW64619/42). On the right is the steamship *Ollanta* which plied (then) a weekly overnight passenger and freight service from Puno in Peru.

Above: A Flandes and Giradot train *en route* from the small town of Buenos Aires behind Baldwin 2-8-2 No. 47 in August 1987. The engine is Baldwin works No. 60569/28 and is normally kept at Flandes for uncertain freights between there and a cement factory at Buenos Aires. It is a fine specimen of a narrow-gauge Baldwin engine of the interwar years, very reminiscent of the greater days of the Colorado narrow-gauge systems.

Right: The river bridge at Giradot in eastern Colombia, with Baldwin 2-8-2 No. 47 crossing in August 1987. Little traffic uses this route today.

Incas through to La Paz and, 1,500 miles away, Buenos Aires. Guaqui has a small shed which still uses steam for shunting the port.

Colombia too has a little steam in and around Bogota, with a tourist train on Sundays to Nemacon; the district around Bogota station is very tough and definitely not recommended for the solo visitor. Some three hours south-west into the mountains is Flandes, the last of the Colombian Railways' repair depots, where a selection of hulks rest out in the jungle while desultory overhauls take place on the few steam engines kept in service. A freight service runs on some weekdays to Giradot and on about 35 miles of track to a cement works at Buenos Aires. If steam is used, it is in the form of a 1928 double-framed

Above: Sibambe & Quenca 2-8-0 No. 17 takes a special train up from the reverse at the Devil's Nose *en route* for Alausi. This mountain section of the Guayaquil & Quito Railway (3 ft gauge) is the last South American steam operation over the Andes, bar irregular workings on the narrow-gauge beyond Huancayo in Peru. The photograph was taken in September 1986 when part of the western section was still washed out from severe winter storms and No. 17 was the only steam locomotive available beyond Bucay.

Baldwin 2-8-2 No. 47, and the journey from the works to Giradot takes it over the great bridge spanning the Magdalena River. Care is needed even here, and it is unwise to go alone.

Ecuador, of which more later, still runs steam out of Guayaquil but the mountain section has been the subject of washouts over recent years and the line is cut. Diesels are the norm except on the flat coastal section from Duran (a very rough quarter on the opposite side of the river to Guayaquil) to Bucay, where there is a largish steam-engine depot, these days full of dead engines. Some regular industrial and tourist steam operates in Brazil but Venezuela is too oil-rich for anything but the internal combustion engine.

North and east in strife-torn Central America there is a small residue of steam, though Guatemala is the only country where this is reasonably accessible. Such live steam power as there is can be found at Guatemala City, where a 1947 Baldwin 2-8-2 No. 205 is kept in working order against emergencies and special workings. If you are lucky, down on the steaming Atlantic coast at the end of the 'Atlantico' section No. 204 can be found shunting the docks at Puerto Barrios. The chance of a special is rare indeed but to ride one of these or even a freight up the grades in the mountain section west of Zacapa, 89 miles to the capital, is an experience not to be missed. The 3 ft 0 in gauge line abounds in sharp curves and spindly trestle bridges culminating in the big Puente de las Vacas on entering the shanty-town extremity of Guatemala City. The 'Pacifico' section west of Guatemala City is equally mountainous, with a scenic background of active volcanoes and a 3½ per cent grade from Esquintla. Other seemingly dead engines can be seen around, including a turn-of-the-century Baldwin 2-6-0 No. 34 preserved (and said to be steamable) on one of the centre roads at Guatemala City terminus. The whole line was built and used by the United Fruit Company and consequently all official distances are measured in miles and heights in feet.

Mexico, the U.S.A. and Canada have long lost even their short-line steam, though all run tourist specials, and the States abounds in tourist railways, which are big business. The same applies to Great Britain and most of Western Europe, though Austria has been known to produce an odd Kreigslok 2-10-0 in regular service and Italy certainly has a number of pockets, though sadly the Paola-Cosenza rack line has recently closed. Italian steam tends to come out on excursions, which can sometimes be traced in advance by checking with local enthusiast organizations.

The narrow-gauge systems of Portugal once used a magnificent collection of steam power, including smart little compound-tank engines which climbed their twisting ways from the Douro Valley through the vineyards towards the Spanish border. They ran up from junctions with the standard-gauge line out of Oporto, and in September they carried groups of harvesters; whole families, often of three generations, and even entire villages, making teams of as many as 50 or 100 people, would go on their annual outing, like the London East-enders of old for their annual hop-picking in Kent. Little trains headed by spotless 2-4-6-0 Mallet tanks heaved themselves up the vine-clad valley of the Corgo from Regua with a wonderful collection of sounds emerging from their wooden-seated third-class carriages, where groups of villagers with their accordions, guitars, mouth-organs and drums happily envisaged a month of back-breaking but well-paid work ahead of them. Most of the passengers brought (and still bring) their own food, for there are no refreshment rooms except at the main junctions, though perhaps a small wine counter in some odd corner at a country stop might also have an offering of sausage, bread and hard cheese.

The little compound locos with their attractive copper-capped chimneys may still come out at busy times but the days are now gone where their presence can be taken for granted, for

Opposite: A special excursion crosses a spindly trestle bridge on the Atlantico section of FEGUA, the Guatemala State Railways. The engine, with an additional water tender because of poor supplies *en route* to Guatemala City, is 2-8-0 No. 205, a Baldwin of 1947. The line built in conjunction with the United Fruit Company is 3 ft 0 in gauge and almost 100 per cent dieselized. Some steam is kept at depots around the country but in August 1987 No. 47 was one of two operable engines.

Right: A class 75 2-8-2 belonging to the JZ (Yugoslav State Railway) 760 mm narrow-gauge railway once running from Belgrade to Dubrovnik via Sarajevo waits with a passenger train at Titovo Uzice in the early 1970s. Two classes of locomotives were used for adhesion work on this very scenic line, the 85 class 2-8-2 and the 83 class 0-8-2. All steam is now gone, as has most of the railway.

Opposite: Under the supervision of the FCC (Cuban State Railways) signal tower, Mogul No. 1606 (Vulcan W3143/20) crosses the main line with a load of sugar cane for the Boris Luis S. Coloma sugar mill on 15 February 1987.

Below: Regua station on the Douro Valley line out of Oporto with a 2-4-6-0 Mallet tank at the head of a late afternoon mixed train for Vila Real and Chaves in April 1970. The broad-gauge platforms are to the right of the metre-gauge bay. At that time all services over this narrow-gauge branch were in the hands of these spotlessly kept Mallets.

diesel railcars do most of the work without difficulty. At least one of the Mallets has gone to happier climes, purchased to run in tandem with a French (ex-Reseau Breton) 2-6-0 tank over a *route touristique*, the Chemins de Fer de Provence out of Nice north towards Alpine foothills at Digne.

Steam comes up every now and again in Yugoslavia but that wonderful two-day trek by 760 mm narrow-gauge train from the outskirts of Belgrade to Sarajevo, a full day's journey, has gone.

Within the last decade this and the section containing the rack line between Rastelica and Bradina, across the arid scrub-covered mountains and down to Dubrovnik, have given way to a new standard-gauge line. But even in the halcyon days photography was difficult, for in the area of Bosnia, Herzegovina and Dalmatia there was always paranoia about railway photography – one of the last countries in Europe except Bulgaria to be so inclined. As far back as 1962 when the author was working for the BBC and in possession of permits, the team was hauled in for interrogation by the police. But those were great days; finishing our filming we would return down the steep grades to Dubrovnik on an evening freight, with an engine on the front and rear, trundling off into the evening as a golden sun lowered itself into the blue-black Adriatic. Dumping our gear in the despatcher's office, we would walk across the small yard to bathe in the warm sea, alongside the engine shed with our train engines standing on the ash pit. If you trod water you could see the whole Dubrovnik railway scene, with perhaps another freight for Hum and Sarajevo barking its way up into the darkness, its engines whistling like banshees.

THE SUGAR ISLANDS

Cuba, the Philippines, Java, Sumatra: the thought of visiting any of these exotic islands sets the steam enthusiast's heart beating fast. Even today there are probably in the region of 500 serviceable steam locomotives in action on Castro's island, over 95 per cent of which are of U.S. design and manufacture. Gauges range from standard down through 3 ft to 2 ft 3 in, with 2 ft 6 in the most popular of the narrow-gauge systems. You can even go it alone if you keep a low profile, hire a car (expensive because there is no unlimited mileage) and keep to the cane fields, not the mills. But it is probably better to go in an organized group, for then Minaz (the Cuban abbreviation for Ministry and Sugar) will, after much bureaucracy, take care of you, allowing entry to a very new world – or perhaps a very old one – of Alcos, Baldwins, Cookes and Vulcans, to name but the most prolific of American manufacturers. The time of major activity is February and March, when the sugar mills are at their busiest. Today the mills carry the names of revolutionary heroes, though the word 'Central' (meaning the sugar factory itself) still appears consistently. Most of the steam power now active in Cuba was delivered to the plantations new, and rather sadly most of the second-hand locomotives once used on American mainland short lines have gone – probably purged from the plantations prior to Castro's time. A great deal of this equipment had been sold to the sugar lines by three big southern States dealers, Southern Iron and Equipment, Birmingham Rail and Locomotive, and Georgian Car and Locomotive.

Cuba is a large island and many of the cane fields cover a huge area, with locomotives working as far as 15 miles away from their base shed adjacent to the main mill. In addition there is a considerable amount of working over the FCC (National Railways) trackage. Some of the cane-field lines even operate a workmen's passenger service, using either cane cars or light

Above: Alco Cooke 2-8-0 No. 1549 (62620/10/20) brings a fully loaded train of sugar cane down the main line adjacent to the mill on the C. Marcelo Salado system on 18 February 1985. This standard-gauge railway owns two consolidations (both Alco-Cookes), a 4-6-0 and a Mogul (both Baldwins), all in sparkling external order. The line is 28 miles long.

Right: C. Marcelo Salado 0-4-0 saddle tank, a Davenport of unrecorded vintage but beautifully clean like all its sisters in the mill's fleet, shunts the mill-yard at Reforma on 18 Feburary 1985.

Left: No. 1357, a Baldwin consolidation (33553/7/09), shunts the mill-yard on the 2 ft 6 in gauge C. Pepito Tey in February 1985. This railway has a classic assortment of Baldwin narrow-gauge power (four consolidations and three moguls) dating from 1909 to 1924. There is talk of the system being converted to standard gauge in the near future.

Below: Humberto Alvarez Baldwin No. 9, a 2-8-0 built in 1925, struggles mightily back to the mill on 1 March 1957. This somewhat isolated 2 ft 6 in gauge line traverses rolling hills in Matanzas Province, using Baldwin and Vulcan 2-6-0s and 2-8-0s.

four-wheel railcars which buck and sway over the usually indifferent track in the manner of an old-time light railway.

One of the finer standard-gauge systems is the Marcelo Salado, which has a venerable collection of engines kept in tip-top condition, with white-tyred wheels and black livery with yellow lining and numerals. Trains can be hauled by magnificent Baldwin 4-6-0s or Alco 2-8-0s – and these are *proper* trains, the engines carrying white marker flags and the whole train ending with a caboose. These trains operate on the FCC for approximately three miles to the junction with their own branch. In contrast, the narrow-gauge lines are likely to be in a much poorer condition, though there are some shining examples, such as the 2 ft 6 in gauge Pepito Tey where the little Baldwin 2-6-0s and 2-8-0s have very tall chimneys, giving them an old-fashioned timeless air, or Espartaco with its outside-framed Baldwin 2-8-0s and a pair of fireless engines (0-4-2 Porter and 0-4-0 Orenstein & Koppel). Many of the mills have been active since the mid-1800s, and over 130 of them have railroads today, making it almost impossible to see or list everything. Among the treasures undoubtedly to be found are Baldwins

almost a century old setting out with four-wheeled cane trucks into the rolling hills and palm trees. And although it is not steam, a sight not to be missed in Cuba is the Hershey Railway, an all-electric standard-gauge line, probably the only example left of an 'all American' inter-urban electric; it has been left virtually untouched from the bad old days.

It should also be mentioned that, as in Cuba, the sugar-cane industry in Brazil produced its railways, mainly in the Campos north-east of Rio. Although the use of rail haulage here is getting less and less, there are still swaying and creaking lines, and you may find Baldwin 2-8-0s of 1894, Armstrong Whitworth 4-6-0s of 1920 and Porter 2-6-0s.

Opposite and left: The Ciro Redondo system is one of the larger standard-gauge railways operating in Cuba, using a batch of Alco and (mostly) Baldwin consolidations, all of them over 60 years old. This is a huge, well-run operation. No. 1828, a Baldwin 2-8-0 (52970/2/20), is seen here in the environs of the mill on 19 February 1985.

Overleaf top: One of the cleanest and mechanically well-kept engines in Cuba, Baldwin Mogul (58654/9/25) No. 1530 rests on the shed at Progreso on the afternoon of 17 February 1985. Behind is Porter 0-4-0 saddle tank No. 1121. This short, 15-mile standard-gauge line also owns Vulcan and two Baldwin 2-6-0s in addition to two Porter ancients, both 0-4-0 tanks.

Overleaf bottom: Two ten-wheelers, a Baldwin (works number unknown but built in 1919) and an Alco (54836/5/14), C. George Washington's Nos. 1643 and 1632, finish their day's work on 20 February 1985. The other working engine that day was Baldwin 2-6-0 (58132/12/24) No. 1557.

Left: The Hershey Railway (standard gauge) is a magnificent example of an American inter-urban system and a living monument to all those lines once running in most parts of the United States. This photograph was taken at the Havana terminus (strictly Casa Blanca, on the opposite side of the estuary to Havana) in February 1985. Still very much alive, the Hershey system with its conductors and motormen in U.S.A. style uniforms (if somewhat moth-eaten) provides a busy local service even though the tracks can be overgrown with grass.

51

One of the blue and yellow 0-6-0 Baldwins, belonging to the 3 ft 0 in gauge Hawaiian Philippine Co., shunts at a siding while out in the cane fields on 15 February 1983. This 93-mile-long line is one of the better kept railways on Negros island even though it had to be totally rehabilitated after the Japanese occupation in the Second World War. The engine is No. 7 and carries the name *Edwin B. Herkes*.

After Cuba, the next best steam attraction, particularly for Americans, must be the Philippines, where the island of Negros not only has a number of sugar lines hard at work but also has in use on one of them the last of the dinosaurs – a real, working Shay. Negros is just over an hour's flight from Manila, and at Bacolod City there is a reasonable hotel which boasts a form of rattling air conditioning – very necessary, for sugar grows in places where it is very hot indeed. Bacolod was built from sugar profits in the 1920s and though fading fast still retains something of its colonial past, with a vast Catholic church set in the midst of a decaying midwest atmosphere; American disco music and cola are today's trappings.

Mills within easy reach of Bacolod include Victorias, which has an extensive system using well-kept green-painted engines on the 2 ft gauge, mostly Henschel 0-8-0 tender tanks but also, wonder of wonders, two 0-4-4 tanks by Bagnall which came from Hong Kong, once used on the Kowloon-Canton Railway Fan-ling branch. Another excellent line is the Hawaiian Philippines, this time a 3 ft gauge operation with Henschel and Baldwin 0-6-0s of 1920 vintage. Sadly, however, many of the mills are shut, their extensive collection of motive power silent, some rusting away never to be steamed again.

Once upon a time Mallets and the geared Shay locomotives were used extensively on the Philippines sugar-

The 3 ft 0 in gauge Lopez Sugar Central on Negros island still has one working geared locomotive, Shay No. 10, built by Lima and used as a standby for diesels as well as at peak periods. It is seen here out in the cane fields on 16 February 1983.

cane and logging lines, as both types were designed to spread axle loads over poorly laid track. The last working Shay belongs to Lopez Sugar Central and is a 3 ft gauge engine; in happier days she worked in Missouri over standard-gauge tracks. Today on a dieselized railway, No. 10 only comes out at peak times or when there are problems. The Shay propels its train from the mill-yard up into the cane fields, working flat out, and though the gears reduce speed to around 10 mph it still sounds like 70. Riding up on this train, a fantastic experience on a wagon next to the locomotive's smokebox, one forgets the rather obvious poor maintenance, the dubious boiler examinations, cracked stays and low water-levels.

So far it is the price of oil that keeps the Philippine steam engines going. A practice of make do and mend has kept them just about alive, though grave-yards abound all over Negros island. In contrast to Cuba, steam here is in rough shape and cannot go on for ever. Their steam engines are called 'Drag-ons' and maybe that is just what they are, though these examples are thank-fully not quite extinct.

Last, but by no means least, are the little lines of the spice islands, Java and Sumatra, all very much alive even in the late 1980s. Java alone is reported to have around 50 sugar-cane railways, plus many others serving forestry areas and palm plantations. Salawasi (for-merly Celebes) had a public tramway prior to the Second World War and although this is now closed it is rumoured that portions may still

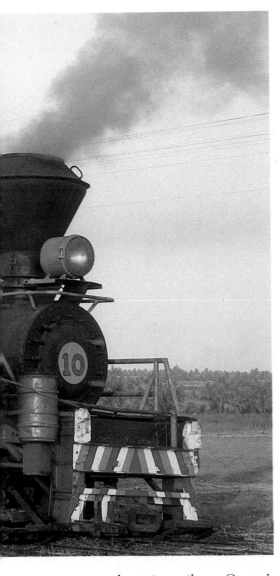

operate as a plantation railway. Central and eastern Java and north Sumatra are the main areas for these small railways, often of 600 mm or 700 mm gauge. Locomotives used on them are varied, to say the least – almost as varied as those once used on the main-line systems. Probably the 0-8-0 tender tank predominates, as it does in the Philippines, though this is followed by a much more exotic type, the 0-4-4-0T Mallet.

On the whole the systems are not large but as one seeks out elusive main-line steam early in the morning, a small green, blue or yellow steam engine may often appear out of the cane fields and run for miles alongside the rough road *en route* to pick up sugar further down the line. In north Sumatra the traffic is heavy on the palm-oil plantations, with over 100 engines, many of them gorgeous Mallet tanks, spread around just seven oil estates. It has recently been stated that there must be at least 500 narrow-gauge industrial steam engines at work in Indonesia for those who are hardy enough to seek them out. Some are German, some Dutch, some British dating from the 1920s, but amazingly enough there is a British Hunslet 0-4-2 saddle tank of 1971, one of the last ever to be built.

The children's saying 'sugar and spice and all things nice' certainly applies to these exotic islands. But it is only a matter of time before the mutter and reek of the diesel takes over. Exploration is only for the most hardy of railway enthusiasts, but while it lasts, here is a whole new world of old working steam.

The La Carlotta system, again on Negros island, runs some steam in the peak cutting season but most of the black-painted engines on this 3 ft 0 in gauge railway appeared in a poor state on 28 March 1986. This Baldwin 0-6-0 tender tank (extra order 987/31 although carrying a works plate 58940/25) was restricted to yard use only and is seen here taking on long thin strips of wood as fuel. Its La Carlotta number is 105.

Above: Central and eastern Java are the main areas for the sugar railways, which even today can be seen hard at work using a fascinating variety of motive power. Most are 600 mm and 700 mm gauge. This Orenstein & Koppel tank, mill No. 10, was photographed at Purwodadi in August 1975.

Opposite: Gernrode station on the metre-gauge Selketalbahn in the Harz mountains, September 1983. In the station is 0-4-4-0 Mallet tank No. 99.5906 (Karlsruhe/1918) on the second train of the day to Hasselfelde, using the recently built section between Strassenberg and Guntersberge. This links with the line to Nordhausen, worked by the more standard DR metre-gauge 2-10-2 tanks.

EASTERN EUROPE AND THE EDGE OF ASIA

Deep in the wooded valleys of the Harz mountains in East Germany there are more living dinosaurs. As the September sun clears the hilltops and the morning mist disperses over the roofs of the small town, the station at Gernrode comes to life. Opposite the single-platformed terminus is a small engine shed housing a stubby boilered 2-6-2 tank and a couple of the 99.59 class 0-4-4-0 Mallet tanks used over this section of the metre-gauge network. These Mallets are the last of their type to be found in regular service anywhere and, in spite of rumours to the contrary, no diesel trials have yet taken place. Brown briquette smoke drifts from the tapered stovepipe chimney as No. 99.5901 moves gently out of the shed watched by the local policeman, who has stopped to cast an eye over the foreign enthusiast whose

camera is at the ready. But there are no problems here for the East German authorities look benignly on the rail fan who behaves himself. The Mallet picks up her coaches and drifts into the station platform, then takes water while waiting for the time to start her journey up the bank through the chestnut forests to Alexisbad. A couple of years ago a Mallet tank failed to make it when the 11.00 Gernrode to Harzgerode got its central buffer interlocked with the leading coach on the passing loop at Magdesprung: a squad of mechanics duly arrived by motorcycle and discovered a damaged coupling. Passengers were then invited to walk to Alexisbad.

The Harzquerbahn is only one section of several isolated East German narrow-gauge lines, all steam-worked; quite contrary to other such systems once in operation in Western Europe they have been modernized, and they prosper. The majority use a standard series of powerful 2-10-2 tanks, some

Right: A passenger train from Ganzhad to Kurot Oberweisenthal approaches Kretscham behind metre-gauge 2-10-2 tank No. 99 1777.4 during a weekend in June 1978. This is a steeply graded line which the powerful 2-10-2 tanks take in their stride.

Opposite bottom: Saxon Meyer 0-4-4-0 tank No. 99 1606.5 at Wolkenstein in June 1983 making ready for the morning train to Niederschmeideberg and Johstadt. By the middle of 1986 the latter section was closed, with that to Niederschmeideberg following early in 1987 after improvements to the parallel road.

dating back to pre-Second World War days but most constructed in more recent years. Apart from the Nordhausen end of the Harzquerbahn-Selketalbahn (the two systems were linked as late as 1985), other lines serve the hilly wooded countryside, including the long Zittau-Jonsdorf line which, besides freight traffic, clearly picks up a purposeful tourist trade. That elite magazine of overseas railway enthusiasts, *The Continental Railway Journal*, reported in 1986 that the Radebeul Ost-Radeberg section normally worked by the ever-present 2-10-2 tanks held a special day in September 1985 when not only was the restored 'Traditionzug' running but also a 'Traditionzug-Extrazug'! With regular staff helped out by enthusiasts, a real holiday atmosphere prevailed. Staff and many of the passengers were dressed in period costume, an open coach transported an 'oompah' band and Mitropa, the State Railway refreshment and sleeping car operation,

dispensed beer from a seemingly inexhaustible stock in the depths of the brake-van at every (lengthy) station stop. The engine for the Traditionzug was one of the Saxon Meyer 0-4-4-0 tanks, while the Extrazug used a Saxon 0-10-0 tank. Who says communist countries are dull?

The green Saxon Mayers are beautiful survivors of a bygone age; in appearance they are like Mallets only with cylinders back to back – another form of articulated engine. Until 1986 their more famous haunts were on the metre-gauge section from Wolkenstein to Johstadt via Niederschmeideberg, where unsuitable roads kept the line open until Dresden decided otherwise. This charmingly rural line carried freight from the junction at Wolkenstein by means of transporter wagons, the main-line vehicles riding piggyback in similar fashion to the Leek and Manifold Railway in England many years ago. While the Wolkenstein line has now gone, the Meyers still run

the Oschatz-Muglen-Kemmlitz section, though care is needed if photographing here as there is a nearby military barracks.

East Germany can still be a steam enthusiast's paradise for although the great Pacifics no longer run, there are steam centres galore, including Saalfeld (which actually retains a 'Tradition Pacific'), Halberstadt Gorlitz and Zittau with an overall variety of 2-10-0s, 2-8-2s and large 2-8-4 tanks. Such is the popularity of steam that the Saalfeld Pacific 01.1531 regularly works specials at weekends.

In addition there are the narrow-gauge systems with their modern and fascinating elderly motive power, particularly the Mallet tanks in the Herz mountains.

Above: Saxon Meyer 0-4-0 + 0-4-0 No. 99.1585 takes the morning train from Wolkenstein to Johstadt as the mist begins to clear one October morning in 1982. These unique locomotives worked all the services on this narrow-gauge line of the DR until closure in 1987 after considerable road improvements in the area. Service was reasonably brisk with separate passenger and freight services, the latter mainly to and from Niederschmeideberg.

The 09.35 passenger train to Niederschmeideberg and Johstadt on the latter section in June 1983. The locomotive is Saxon Meyer 0-4-4-0 tank No. 99 1606.5. A separate passenger and freight service worked over this 760 mm gauge line, the freight train using transporter wagons for standard-gauge vehicles.

A class 50 2-10-0 No. 50.3698 approaches Reifland with train No. 64325, Hilkersdorf to Pockau-Lengfield, on 2 August 1985. This is a standard design of freight locomotive for German Railways which could once be seen from the Baltic to Vienna.

Overleaf top: The afternoon train from Schlettau to Crottendorf behind spotlessly clean 2-8-2 tank No. 86.1501 in June 1983. Both the engines of this class used on the lines, Nos. 86.1501 and 86.1001, were kept in prime condition and were highly regarded by their crews, one locomotive taking the morning stint and the second the afternoon, changing over at Annaberg-Buchholz.

Overleaf bottom: East German DR 2-8-2 No. 411.1263 at Saalfeld in June 1978. At that time Saalfeld was also home to the 01 Pacifics as well as standard class 50 2-10-0s and the 95 class 2-8-2 tanks.

Preceding page: DT 2-8-2 tank No. 95.0045 climbs up into the hills towards the West German border with the 16.50 from Saalfeld to Sonneberg on a June evening in 1978. Some ten minutes after taking this photograph the author was stopped by the police for being too close to the border and fined – in West German marks.

Opposite: New and (only relatively) old stand side by side at Kaposvar, Hungary in June 1978. On the left is diesel shunter No. M31.2014, while on the right is one of the modern 424 class 4-8-0s No. 424.142 used on both passenger and freight services prior to electrification and dieselization. At the time this photograph was taken steam was very much in use at Kaposvar, including the 424 class tender engines, with 2-6-2 tanks and 2-4-2 tanks on local services.

Above right: Plovdiv station in August 1974; the engine is ex-German 2-10-0 No. 14.35. Very little steam was working on Bulgarian State Railways' standard gauge by the mid-1970s.

Right: Cervenbreg station with a train about to depart behind 2-10-2 tank No. 607.76 on the 760 mm branch. This line to Orjahavo was one of two Bulgarian narrow-gauge lines operating in 1974 but the only one still using steam. The 76 class 2-10-2 tanks worked all services, which were mixed when required.

Other parts of Eastern Europe are not quite so friendly towards the railway enthusiast, though there are signs of a thaw in Czechoslovakia (once extremely difficult) and Hungary where, alas, regular steam is over: the relaxation has come ten years too late. Both countries have kept active locomotives and run these from time to time. Unfortunately, the quest for photographing steam in the Eastern bloc has always been fraught with problems, though no rail fan worthy of the name has failed to obtain adequate pictures. Poland is still very steamy indeed and though organized parties are welcomed, there are strict limits as to exactly what can and cannot be photographed. Most railway buildings, no matter how insignificant, come under the ban and it is even uncertain if railway photography is allowed in the open countryside with no buildings – 'strategic' or otherwise – in sight. Even

Steam is still well in evidence on secondary lines throughout Poland and ex-German class 52 2-10-0s predominate more than 40 years after their introduction during the Second World War. Known in Poland as class TY2, these engines are common in the hilly south where they are often used on quite lengthy trips without turning. One such route is that from Chabowka to Nowy Sacz where the TY2 will have a tender-first journey of nearly 80 km. The photograph was taken near Kasina Weilka in April 1987.

when permits *are* given, photographers are likely to be accompanied by policemen who prevent any pictures being taken where backgrounds are in their view 'strategic'; these might include turntables, locomotive shed buildings or any form of marshalling yard.

Poland is nevertheless a popular place for the railway enthusiast, with many visits arranged. There is still a great variety of steam working both passenger and freight trains, though like in East Germany the days of the Pacifics are over. In addition to the main line there are a number of 760 mm narrow-gauge railways worked for the most part by PX 48 and PX 49 class 0-8-0s. However, steam in Poland, though massive by comparison with most countries, is now in full retreat, with some classes of steam locomotives near to extinction, including the once famous Pt 47 2-8-2 – the last express passenger steam locomotive in Europe.

The only acknowledged steam in Soviet Russia is likely to be one of the 'Pioneer' railways – narrow-gauge lines, mostly in parks, introduced (also in the satellite countries) with the serious object of training young people in how to run a railway, though today most railways are dieselized. Nevertheless, a trip across Russia from the Chinese border through Moscow to Leningrad in 1986 exposed not only vast quantities of dumped steam engines but also some which were very much alive, including 2-10-0s shunting at Ulan Ude, Irkutsk and Zabaikalsk, while others, among them 0-8-0s and 0-10-0s, lurked darkly in sheds. Most of these engines were somewhat unkempt, although Sverdlovsk obviously had a station pet, which was maintained in pristine condition and headed a short train used to refuel the samovars of the Beijing to Moscow express among others. But sadly the Su 2-6-2s with their high running plates and the massive P36 4-8-4s are gone, unless they are being kept on some secret strategic reserve.

Left: Two engines simmer in the darkness at Klodzko shed on 4 September 1984; on the turntable is class TKT48 2-8-2 tank No. 39, while to its right in a well-lit stall another 2-8-2, this time class PT47, awaits its turn of duty. This south-west corner of Poland has remained a steam centre for some years.

Below: Poland is notorious for bad weather but occasionally the clouds clear to give a scene reminiscent of a South African winter. This was so on the morning of Easter Sunday 1987 when an unknown class TY2 2-10-0 was climbing through the Silesian hills near Lachowice with the 05.54 train from Sucha Beskidzka to Zywiec, south of Cracow.

69

Classic P36 class 4-8-4 No. P36.0030 with the west-bound 'Russia' about to depart from Kharbarovsk, Siberia, on 15 November 1970. Introduced as late as 1953, these powerful machines, cabs totally enclosed to cope with the Russian winter, came into production between 1954 and 1956, and for nearly 20 years handled the famous Trans-Siberian trains, including the 'Russia' and the through services to Mongolia and China. Some of the class were finished in blue livery similar to the streamlined 4-6-4s but the majority, smartly kept, bore the standard light green livery with dignity.

The P36 was a post-Second World War engine that emerged from the works in batches between 1954 and 1956, and became the world's most numerous class of 4-8-4, handling the legendary cross-Russia trains with ease and distinction. Their last years on the Siberia section east of Irkutsk were times to remember. Who could fail to sit enthralled as the long train of green coaches headed by one of these monsters heaved and twisted its way up over the grades between the silver birches beyond the wind-swept shores of Lake Baikal? Like on earlier journeys in Canada, winter was the most dramatic time to travel, with the train ice-encrusted amid a landscape of endless snow and stark leafless trees – then came the curves with a view ahead and a plume of pure white steam, as the P36 thundered on from division to division.

There are a number of locomotives preserved, including the class U 4-6-0 at Moscow's Pavelets station – its life having been saved by hauling Lenin's funeral train in 1924. The Russians do

Left: Over 1,900 'Russian Decapods' were built in the U.S.A during the Second World War and sent to Russia under the 'head-lease' agreement. These YE class locomotives were used exclusively in Siberia and No. E 3068 was photographed at Talden from the vestibule door of a sleeping car on train No. 1, *Rossiya*, on 16 November 1970. Crossing Russia by train today (even though steam does not officially exist) one comes across the odd working 2-10-0 belonging to classes YEa and YEm and in March 1986, at least, the SZD (Russian State Railway) evidently still had over 1,000 of their American-built locomotives classed as serviceable. Other classes seen by the author as late as 1987 include the L 2-10-0 and LV 2-10-2.

Bottom: TCDD (Turkish State Railways) 2-8-2 No. 46104 (Robert Stephenson 3996/1929), ex-Otterman Railway 133, stands at Odemis in April 1977 having worked the daily local from Izmir. A later member of the class, No. 46105, the last survivor, and completely non-standard on today's Turkish system, received a major overhaul in May 1987 with its boiler good for a further 12 months. The Izmir (Alsancak) to Odemis twice weekly mixed train is the principal reason for the longevity of the class.

Overleaf top: Although steam is officially finished in Turkey, the intrepid explorer is still likely to find some activity, especially in winter, as can be seen here with 2-10-0 No. 56159 climbing above the snow-line towards Soglani heading train No. 1922, the 05.33 daily mixed from Ezurum to Kars on 3 April 1986.

not encourage contacts with Western railway enthusiasts and the traveller is advised to be extremely circumspect in note-taking.

One of the last of the steam lover's paradises has been Turkey where, although steam has now officially finished, pockets still come alive, especially in the winter. A party visiting this country in 1987 found a *newly overhauled* 1932 Robert Stephenson-built 2-8-2, the only survivor of its class, back at work in its old haunts on the Izmir to Odemis branch – a misnomer in British terms as it is a day's journey out and back! Other steam engines still kicking quite hard include 2-10-2s, 0-8-0s and the German Kreigslok 2-10-0s. The latter engines, a class once found all over wartime occupied Europe, originally came to a neutral Turkey as a 'come on' from the Germans, hoping to influence her to enter the war on the side of the Axis powers. The British also made overtures, sending a number of Stanier-designed 2-8-0s which had to make the journey out via the Cape and the Suez

Right: A special train
was chartered by the
London travel firm, Jules
Verne, in September 1985.
The idea was to travel by
train all the way from
London's Charing Cross
station to Xian in China to
celebrate 2,100 years of the
Silk Road; where possible
steam was used, including
some sections across
Turkey. Nicknamed the
Million Dollar Expressi
because of the cost of this
luxury journey, the train,
already very late, is seen
here in full cry near Irmak
on 29 September, heading
for the Russian border.
Motive power is provided
by a pair of Skyliner
2-10-0s led by No. 56302.

Canal. Because of mines and attacks on shipping in the Mediterranean at that time, parts had to be dumped on various islands before final shipment to the Turkish State Railways. Two experts from Derby were sent out to Ankara to superintend the erection of the engines, which became nicknamed the Churchills. One of these Stanier 2-8-0s was actually seen in steam as late as 1987. Some of the finest railway photographs of recent years have been taken in Turkey with its hilly country and sharp clear atmosphere, particularly during the autumn and the dry winter. But steam-trackers should note that trying to chase trains by car is a hazardous experience with Turkish road traffic and European visitors doing this, particularly in the east, may lay themselves open to unwelcome attention. However, with a Turkish speaker in tow there really are delights to be had, footplate rides included.

Above: Ex-German wartime 2-10-0 No. 56523 waits at Afyon at the head of train 1762, the 07.05 to Usak and Alasehir, in April 1985. Like most of the Turkish local trains this is a 'mixed'.

Overleaf: On 23 September 1985, 0-10-0 No. 55024 heads up the branch from Isparta with the 17.30 to Bozanonu.

73

Above: The 07.55 local passenger train from Samsun to Azot makes its way close to the Black Sea coast on 31 March 1986. The locomotive is 2-8-0 No. 45062.

Right: British-built (Robert Stephenson) 2-8-2 No. 46102, the duty pilot, and German (Henschel) 4-6-4 tank No. 3705, resplendent in green livery and waiting to work the 17.30 local train to Alasehir, stand on the shed at Manisa in April 1977. The 4-6-4 tanks once worked the suburban services out of Istanbul prior to electrification.

Further south, strife-torn Lebanon is likely to number a lost railway among its problems, which is sad because the 1005 mm gauge Damascus to Beirut line used a rack section out of that beleaguered city with some Swiss-built steam 0-10-0 tanks storming up towards the Beidar Pass. Yet steam survives, if only just, in Syria. The old Hedjaz Railway (which once began in Haifa) normally uses a railcar from Damascus to Dera'a, though every now and again a 2-6-0 tank ventures out with a train of four or five wooden coaches as far as Seighaya on the Lebanese border. The Hedjaz line (also 1005 mm gauge) runs through from Damascus to Dera'a but because of the recent troubles it no longer continues to Amman, though the Hartmann

Above: A TCCD class 56 2-10-0 climbs towards the 2,130 m (7,000 ft) contour as it leaves Topdagi with the daily mixed to Kars in September 1985. This standard two-cylinder mixed traffic class was first delivered from Henschel in 1937 and continued to be built until 1949 by various German manufacturers plus Skoda in Czechoslovakia.

Left: In the kinder years of the early 1970s the rack line out of Beirut on the Lebanese section of the nominally metre-gauge line to Damascus was still working and with it the Swiss-built 0-10-0 tanks.

Steam still survives, if only just, in Syria but in 1974 times were better. A German-built Hartmann 2-8-2 No. 282 takes a 1005 mm gauge train out of Damascus on the Hedjaz line on 27 December 1974.

2-8-2s are still in action between Dera'a and Bosra. A recent report on these made interesting reading: apparently the driver of 2-8-2 No. 260 had been sent to Germany to learn to drive diesels in 1966/67, since when he had worked with nothing but steam in Syria. The true seeker after steam can never believe that all is lost.

AFRICA

In today's world no one can say that African train travel is less exciting than it used to be, though the enthusiast searching for steam will certainly find it less attractive. There are, too, some countries where visitors are no longer welcomed, as they were only a few years back. Uganda, Angola, Mozambique and to an extent Zambia must be crossed off the slate, which is sad since all these countries had a great deal to offer the steam lover. In the very early 1970s it was easy enough to travel over the magnificent British-built (and partly British-owned) Benguela Railway out of Lobito behind Garratts fired on eucalyptus wood home-grown alongside the track – sitting in a leather-chaired wood-panelled diner at that. In those days the Benguela was a prosperous railway carrying copper west from its source in Central Africa, train upon train of it moving in an almost endless stream to the coast. The outward and mechanical condition of its engines reflected the affluence, both in the Garratts and the beautifully proportioned North British-built 4-8-2s which worked the coastal section and the passenger services east beyond Nova Lisboa. You could also have a trip behind one of the Mozambique Atlantics (the last active specimens in the world) from Nampula, or take a ride on the narrow-gauge railway out of Joao Belo on the muddy Limpopo River.

Even during the Rhodesian war, there were interesting railway activities at the border between Victoria Falls (Rhodesia) and Livingstone (Zambia) across the Victoria Falls bridge. Zambia badly needed South African and Rhodesian foodstuffs, and an outlet for her copper exports in exchange, and since the Benguela Railway was out of action by then, a compromise was reached by which the Rhodesian Garratt ran round its train at Victoria Falls station, backing it down to the bridge with most of the wagons over the midspan border line, unhooking and returning to base; a Zambian diesel then collected the wagons once a decent interval of time had elapsed. This was the only regular communication between the stationmasters of Victoria Falls and Livingstone. The same thing happened but in reverse with the exported copper. It was a question of priorities.

Victoria Falls bridge in March 1977, during the last days of Rhodesia's unilateral state of independence. Although there was no official contact between Rhodesia and Zambia at that time, traffic still moved between the two countries taking essential foods into Zambia and bringing out its copper exports. This was achieved by the Rhodesia Railways' locomotive propelling its train down to the bridge and pushing most of the wagons over the white line at the centre of the arch into Zambian territory. The Zambians used the same tactics in reverse. The photograph shows a Rhodesian Garratt collecting a Zambian train which has been positioned in this way.

Preceding page top: One of the magnificent North British Locomotive Co. 4-8-2s of the 3 ft 6 in gauge Benguela Railway at Lobito with the daily through train to Nova Lisboa and Silva Porto in August 1973. The engine came off at Benguela station and a Garratt was substituted for the heavy climb up to the eastern plateau. This was a full dining and sleeping car train taking over 12 hours to reach Nova Lisboa.

Preceding page bottom: An Alco 2-8-0 on the narrow-gauge line out of Joao Belo west of Maputo (Lourenco Marques) and on the banks of the Limpopo River. This busy line used both Baldwin and Alco locomotives dating back to the 1920s.

Until very recently the 3 ft 6 in gauge South Africa Railways has been a mecca for the enthusiast; not only was there steam in abundance but trains also ran through superb scenery headed by a variety of classes, including Garratts and huge class 25NC 4-8-4s. This is not to mention the attractive narrow-gauge lines in Natal. Even five years ago some people considered that steam had a future in the Union, with David Wardale, SAR's Assistant Mechanical Engineer (steam), in the lead with his class 26 4-8-4 No. 3450. Nicknamed *Red Devil*, it was SAR's only locomotive to appear in that colour, aptly projecting a new image. A. E. Durrant,

Above: A huge 3 ft 6 in gauge South Africa Railways' 15F class 4-8-2 heads the Orange Express between Kroonstadt and Bloemfontein nearly two decades ago. Up until the mid-1970s South Africa Railways modernized steam locomotives and electrified more routes, but the diesel lobby has now taken over and the end of steam cannot be far round the corner.

Right: David Wardale leans from the cab as No. 3450 thunders through Olienhoutplaat. The 500th of a second exposure has not quite frozen the action – proof that even with 1,275 tonnes behind the tender, the 5-km climb at 1 in 100 has still not brought speed below the 70 km/h limit imposed on goods trains.

Opposite: The South Africa Railways' passenger trains between Bethlehem and Bloemfontein went diesel on 3 November 1986. Class 25NC 4-8-4 No. 3420 approaches Ionia with the 08.35 Bloemfontein to Bethlehem train on 15 July of that year – almost the end of an era.

A class 25NC 4-8-4 No. 3422 (one of steam's unqualified success stories and dating from 1954) rounds a sharp curve west of Flicksberg with the 08.35 Bloemfontein to Bethlehem passenger train on 12 August 1986.

Right: One of South Africa's 'Baby Garratts', 2-6-2 + 2-6-2 No. NG67, takes water at Lourie on the Avontur line out of Port Elizabeth in July 1971. These engines, built in the U.K., under licence in Germany and as late as 1968 by Hunslet-Taylor in South Africa, monopolized the 2 ft gauge lines of Natal except for the Avontur section, which they shared with the German-built 2-8-2s originating from the South-West African lines prior to standard Cape gauging.

one of the leading experts on SAR matters, recently wrote (in the *Continental Railway Journal*) of a fine run by this engine on the 'Trans Karoo' out of Kimberley. Normally the preserve of two class 34 diesels, the train was headed by No. 3450, and the *Devil* and its driver set out to show that steam could out-perform two diesels. Despite being held back by a sick engine on a preceding freight, it put up a superb performance. After a dead stop at Modderrivier from signals caused by the errant freight, the train bounded along at 110–120 km/h compared with the official road limit of 100 km/h and at Witput, where signals were again at danger, it restarted from a dead stand to 80 km/h in four train lengths. Unfortunately the experiment, though successful, has been to no avail as the CME hierarchy of the SAR have now

decided to dispose of steam traction.

The experimental run was almost a finale for the long-established stronghold of main-line big steam in South Africa, the route from Kimberley to De Aar. Freights and extra passenger trains are still 25NC-hauled at the time of writing but the future must be far from bright.

The last 100 per cent steam-operated main line in South Africa is from Warrenton to Mafeking, the line being worked in two sections, in both cases by class 25NC 4-8-4s. A certain sign of the times has been the disposal (for scrap) of the strategic reserve at De Aar, Touws River and Beaufort West; one stalwart to go was a survivor of the class 25 condensing 4-8-4s, famous machines in their time. There was talk of this engine returning to Glasgow, the city of its birth (it was a North

A class 19D 4-8-2 waits while its hopper wagons discharge into the coal stage at Burgersdorp in March 1977. This spindly trestle approach to the coaling stage is standard South Africa Railways' practice and one where a crew needs a head for heights. Waiting below with a tender full of coal is a spotless class 15AR 4-8-2 used on local passenger trains out of Burgersdorp.

British-built engine), for the transport museum there, but it was not to be. However, the authorities have looked kindly on the preservation movements abroad and have donated two Garratts to Great Britain, one of which is now safely displayed in the Manchester Museum of Science and Industry; it is back in the city of its birth.

The SAR had two types of class 25 4-8-4: the original engines, built from 1953, which had condensing apparatus used to save water while crossing the wastelands of the Karoo, and the later, non-condensing engines (NC). The condensing engines enabled costly watering points between Beaufort West and De Aar to be closed down and obviated the need to haul water to others. Dieselization in the early 1970s provided a better solution to the problem and the class, bar the survivor mentioned above, was converted to 25NC. Many of the engines were worked by regular crews, who kept them in splendid order with all fittings dazzlingly polished, boiler bands gleaming, and who often gave them unofficial names.

This gloom does not mean the imminent end of steam in South Africa. There is some way to go yet, even if the great days are over and gone. There are a few optimistic signs. The Apple Express on the 2 ft gauge out of Port Elizabeth still runs at weekends behind NG15 class 2-8-2s as far as Loerie, and the Alfred Country Railway Committee (a serious group of enthusiasts) is in the process of reopening the Port Shepstone to Harding branch using narrow-gauge Garratt No. NG 88. Until 1987 there were regular long-distance steam rail-tours but their future is in some doubt, though there are regular (almost weekly) well-loaded steam specials on the Johannesburg-Magaliesburg line using the semi-preserved engines out of Millsite shed. Hope has to be the watchword.

Before moving on to the steamy scene in Zimbabwe it is worth a pause to look at its northern neighbour, Zambia. Here the run-down state of the country is not conducive to the

Opposite: Two class 19B 4-8-2s tackle the climb from Rosmead towards the Lootsberg Pass in July 1973; the pilot engine will come off once the summit has been reached. This picture was taken shortly before the Garratts took over the working of this mountainous route.

87

operation of an efficient railway system, but there is a *little* steam in existence. It is generally in poor condition and some locomotives will probably go to Zimbabwe for repair before being sent to Zaire to replace the SAR diesels at present on loan. As things are today very little steam appears to move, though some has been noted on an irregular basis in the Livingstone area, in the form of 20A class 4-8-2 + 2-8-4 Garratts which make the occasional foray to Victoria Falls. Care needs to be taken by railway enthusiasts in Zambia; the cost of taking a few notes may be some hours in a police station.

The news is better in Zimbabwe, much better. Here the railway authorities encourage an interest in their affairs and, what is more, most of the

traffic in the west of the country is moved by steam. Even more exciting is that the motive power is almost exclusively Garratt. There *are* some diesels but the major area of modernization is electrification out of Harare (once Salisbury). The good tidings are that steam is the prime mover for the immediate future, Zimbabwe making good use of its supplies of high-quality coal, while the railway's workshops are geared up to steam locomotive overhaul and maintenance. A large Bulawayo engineering firm (Zeco) are even overhauling Garratts and tank engines from adjacent Mozambique. One of the star places to visit must be Victoria Falls, not only in the hope of seeing a steam train on the spectacular bridge but also for the thrill of the Falls themselves – one of the real Seven

Above: Class 16A 2-8-2 + 2-8-2 No. 606 crosses Crocodile River near Unzimgwane with train No. 84 from Colleen Bawn, on the West Nicholson branch to Bulawayo on 3 August 1986. These smaller eight-coupled Garratts are standard for branch-line working in Zimbabwe.

Opposite: Still beautifully clean in spite of the line having very little traffic, 2-6-2 + 2-6-2 Garratt No. NG 88 passes Renken on the 2 ft 0 in gauge line from Port Shepstone to Harding on 13 August 1986.

Above: One of Rhodesia Railways' (now National Railways of Zimbabwe) 2-6-2 + 2-6-2 Garratts takes water on the shed at Salisbury (Harare) in July 1971, shortly before dieselization of the passenger services.

Right: Class 15A 4-6-4 + 4-6-4 Garratt No. 415 heads an early morning freight train from Thomson Junction off the horseshoe curve above Tajintunda siding on 8 August 1986.

Opposite: NRZ 16A class 2-8-2 + 2-8-2 Garratt No. 609 works hard as it climbs up Mulangwane incline with train No. 314 from Colleen Bawn to Bulawayo on 2 August 1986.

Two of the Wankie Colliery 4-8-2s (similar to Rhodesia Railways' 19th class), numbered 2 and 3, take a heavy train from the mines towards the junction with the then Rhodesia Railways in the winter of 1973. Though not kept in quite such sparkling order today, these engines are still hard at work moving fuel from this huge coalfield.

Wonders of the World. Both the class 15A 4-6-4 + 4-6-4 Garratts, usually found on passenger trains including 'The Mail', and the class 20A eight-coupled Garratts are stationed at Thomson Junction, the main shed for the area; the latter cover heavy freight traffic from the huge Wankie coal mine. Wankie incidentally have their own steam power, green-painted 19th class 4-8-2s, similar to the once numerous 19D class used in South Africa.

Steam is also to be seen in Swaziland,

using ex-SAR 15AR class locomotives, although unfortunately these are somewhat neglected and in far from the pristine condition that they exhibited when in use at Burgersdorp, their last home: very much a case of *sic transit gloria mundi*. Trains work up to the Mozambique border *en route* to Maputo (formerly named Lourenco Marques).

Going north, little is known of any steam in the ex-Belgian Congo, while the Angolan railways are said to be unworkable due to the civil war. Kenya

has gone totally diesel, though recently one of those magnificent 59 class 4-8-2 + 2-8-4 Beyer-Garratts in deep red livery has been restored to full working order for return to the U.K., and No. 5918, *Mount Gelai*, is preserved in working order in Nairobi Railway Museum. These engines, 104 ft long with a 21-ton axle load, were, in their last years, the most powerful steam locomotives in the world, handling 1,200-ton trains up the grades between Mombasa and Nairobi with practised ease. Their successors would have been even larger, in fact the largest Garratts ever designed: 125 ft long with a 25-ton axle load. Unfortunately, the diesels got there first.

West Africa has no steam but the Sudan is a story fit for any revivalist. Like most Third World people the Sudanese were attracted by large offers of aid coming in the form of diesels. These were easy to drive but difficult to maintain, and the usual pattern developed: failures, lack of spares and axle loadings too heavy for badly maintained track. This was very much

Swaziland Railways' hired SAR's class 15AR 4-8-2s at Mlawula in the east of the country, close by the Mozambique border, on 30 July 1986. Shunting on the left is No. 1961, while No. 2096 prepares to take a train westwards to Sidvokodvo. They are a sad sight when one considers the spotless condition of those engines working on their native heath.

the case in the more remote areas, the areas of famine. The distribution of food has forced a revolution – steam has gone back into service.

A weekly mixed train leaves Khartoum on a Monday bound for Babanousa; with luck it will get there by Wednesday. Babanousa is the centre of operations for trains which run west to Nyala and south towards Wau or sometimes east to Sennar, all close to the stricken areas where famine so easily rages. These trains are special for the tracks from Babanousa are light, not taking kindly to diesel axle loadings, while the roads are poor or non-existent especially in the rainy season. A South Wales firm undertook the task of renovating and modernizing the Sudan's engines, which are now moving the traffic helping to feed Africa's starving. Not that this is always easy, for steam here has been dead or at least dying for many years and there is some suspicion of this apparently new-fangled power: farmers have refused to let their sheep be handled by the unknown and trains

A Rhodesia Railways' 12th class 4-8-2 shunting the yard at Bulawayo in July 1971. Traffic was extremely heavy with freights moving out to Harare (Salisbury), Victoria Falls and South Africa. The handsome 12th class engines were used as yard shunters, for trip freights and branch-line passenger services, one taking the overnight mail on from Thomson Junction to Victoria Falls.

have been attacked from time to time. The refurbished engines are the lighter 310 class 2-8-2s; their boilers were sent to the U.K. for heavy repairs through international aid, the rest of the work being carried out in the Sudan.

The story of this amazing turnround goes back to 1983 when Hugh Phillips Engineering, a new firm born from current engineering redundancies, was given the task of compiling a detailed study of steam locomotive rehabilitation in the Sudan. Although a great deal of interest was shown in this report by the Sudan Railways, the project was shelved due to lack of money. However the famine which became world news in 1985 changed the situation; the transport of relief supplies was now an acute problem. By road was difficult or impossible and nearly all the light diesels capable of traversing the lighter rail sections close to the famine areas were out of order – Third World countries may have had diesel aid but they are often unable to afford spares or lack the know-how to

repair the machines. The report was dusted off and Hugh Phillips Engineering was invited by the E.E.C. to assist in the rehabilitation of six steam locomotives to haul relief grain trains over the poorly maintained tracks to Nyala near the Chad border.

The Sudan Railways' workshops at Atbara undertook to overhaul the engine chassis and tenders, while the Welsh company overhauled, or replaced with new, all boiler fittings and ancillaries, and manufactured steam-driven air-compressors and other air-brake system components. The boilers were sent for repair to the company's works at Tredegar on Band Aid grain ships making the return journey. Tools and other necessities for the Atbara works were also supplied, along with technical advice. The resident E.E.C. consultant at Atbara was Bob Watt, ex-British Rail (Scottish Region), who gave the benefit of his wide experience, and Hugh Phillips, Phil Girdlestone and other Tredegar-based staff made regular trips to monitor progress and

95

Above: Sudan Railways' class 310 2-8-2 No. 313 at Berber on its first running in trial in April 1986. Unlike most Sudan Railways' engines, No. 313 has been specially cleaned up for the occasion and the Great Western-style copper cap gleams in the sunshine as the engine is photographed by the E.E.C. consultant overseeing the rejuvenation of six of the engines for use on famine relief trains.

Opposite: The return mixto to Guayaquil waits at Bucay one October afternoon in 1985 loaded to the box-car rooftops – the fare is cheaper that way. Not only passengers but livestock ride on top and it is far from uncommon to see a squealing pig being hauled up on the end of a rope. The engine is Baldwin consolidation No. 44.

highlight problems. The first engine of the six 310 class 2-8-2s, No. 313, was completed in April 1986 and tested before and after fitting a Lempor exhaust designed by Phil Girdlestone. Intended to promote fuel economy and increase power output, this section of the project realized its aims, evaluation being carried out under the close attention of Bob Watt. The remaining five engines, fitted with the new exhaust from the start, were all complete by June 1986 and were shedded at Babanusa, where they duly worked the grain trains to Nyala. Availability generally remained well over 70 per cent and spares were also supplied to restock the empty stores at Atbara and Babanusa.

These locomotives were rebuilt at less than half the unit cost of diesels rehabilitated at the same time, and the difference in the cost of diesel fuel and furnace oil for the steam locomotives (all Sudanese engines are oil-fired) is such that fuel costs for the two types of power are broadly similar. Sudan thus has a lot of lessons to teach developing railways.

SOUTH AMERICA

Guayaquil is Ecuador's second city, a steaming coastal town with handsome boulevards leading to the river front and almost unmentionable poverty elsewhere – not that there is anything unusual about that in South America. What *is* remarkable is that across the muddy estuary of the Rio Guayas, its terminus in the unspeakable Duran, landing place for the small ferry, lurks a working steam railway, the Ferrocarriles Equatorianos or Guayaquil & Quito Railway or, as has been said in scorn (though once in truth), the Good & Quick. Opened in 1903 to link the coast with the capital, the 3 ft 6 in gauge G & Q still survives as a working railway even though a journey by railcar to Quito can take all day while the bus does it in a matter of hours and the plane in one hour.

The ferry bumps into the harbour timbers, while across the dusty way stands a rickety station, also timber-built; it has seen better days, much better. Here, if one searches, is a blackboard with white lettering

Below: Guayaquil & Quito 3 ft 0 in gauge 2-8-0 No. 44, a Baldwin in deep red livery, halts a while *en route* from Bucay to Guayayuin in October 1985 with the daily *mixto* composed of a couple of coaches, assorted box cars and some tank wagons. Although the railway is by no means a tramway, it runs down the main streets of the intermediate towns and villages. Slow but very cheap indeed, this train is almost always steam-headed.

stating '*Trens de Passageros mixto a Riobamba*' run '*todas los dias*' at 6.25 a.m. Helpful if you can read, which many of the inhabitants of Duran certainly cannot. The *mixto* in theory runs to a timetable; anyway, it leaves on time, and what is more, it is usually (even today) steam. Standing among the mass of people on and off the platform in the dark of an equatorial morning, it is hard to see what exactly the train is made up of but it is most likely a number of tank wagons, box cars and possibly two coaches. The passengers ride in and on the roofs of the box cars and coaches; some even ride on the tender of the locomotive. Smaller live produce such as hens can be found in the coaches; larger animals, mostly pigs, are usually hauled on to the roof of a box car.

As the sun slowly rises the Baldwin consolidation (sometimes it can be a more elderly Mogul) rolls its way through the shanty-town suburbs into the tall grasslands, banana plantations and fields of sugar cane *en route* to

Yaguachi, Milagro and, eventually Bucay, where the jungle begins. In each small town the train runs along the middle of the street, ignored by the local inhabitants except those joining or leaving. It is well into midday before the train creeps down the road, locomotive bell clanging, into Bucay; here the engine comes off, turns, and waits after watering for the crew to rest a while before the trip home. Out and back this is a long day for driver, firemen, brakemen and conductor.

After Bucay has been left behind, the track follows the narrow canyon of the Chanchan River, crossing and recrossing the roaring torrent innumerable times over the 27 miles to Sibambe, the line rising 1,500 m (4,950 ft). Once the train reaches this remote junction for the long branch to Cuenca, the whole situation changes for the canyon comes to an abrupt end, blocking the way ahead and leaving as the only means of escape a double switch-back up the sheer mountainside of the 'Devil's Nose'. But even this piece of mountain

An empty stock special approaches Sibambe and the horrendous Devil's Nose reverse on the Guayaquil & Quito Railway in October 1985. This engine is No. 17, a Baldwin 2-8-0 originally belonging to the Sibambe & Quenca Railway which branches off at Sibambe. Behind the train and to its left is the original line washed out in the dreadful winter of 1984.

railway is not the end as there is still a constant climb to the plateau at Palmira, 3,240 m (10,626 ft). In the 50 miles of the Mountain Division the track has risen a total of 3,140 m (10,300 ft) at an average rate of 63 m (206 ft) per mile! From Palmira to Riobamba – the end of any steam operation – the train crosses another 40 miles of rolling paramo.

Today this is one of the few ascents of the Andes available to the rail passenger; certainly no other journey of equal length offers a greater or more fascinating variety than this ride from Guayaquil to Quito. Gone are the days when the weary passenger had to detrain in the evening at Riobamba, stay in what was (and is still) a comfortable hotel and start again at dawn the next day for the capital. Now it is quicker by air, bus or the 'autoferro' railcar – really a bus body on bogies – which at least makes the trip in one day and in daylight. Because of the problem of landslides and the rough terrain trains have never run (officially) in darkness.

Since the rainy season of 1984 nothing has made the complete journey from Bucay to Riobamba for storms have washed away the track in several places, leaving sections, trains and railcars isolated; one long section from Huigra through to Alausi up the 'Devil's Nose' switchbacks and round the stark Alausi loop still operates using a diesel and one coach or, very occasionally, the Cuenca branch engine, a small 2-8-0. Up there in the mountains it is very bleak indeed. In spite of the cost the government is undertaking repairs to and realignments of the track, so it is still possible that the sound of steam will be heard up the 'Devil's Nose' once more – but the repair is a long hard job and another catastrophic rainy season could well be the end.

So, for the present, steam, apart from the isolated Sibambe & Quenca consolidation, is only available on the lower coastal line, where the red Edwardian Moguls and the red or black 1920s consolidations are still part of everyday life; some overhauls

Left: Ex-Sibambe & Quenca consolidation No. 17 leaves Alausi and heads for the mountains towards Riobamba in October 1985. At that time the line was cut a few miles further on due to the bad storm of the previous winter and no other steam power was available, although a shuttle service between Alausi and Huigra was run by a diesel and one coach.

are in hand but most of the motive power lies cold and still in the large shed at Bucay. Maybe the Good & Quick will run its *mixto* to Riobamba again; if so, it will be behind a Baldwin consolidation. If it does not, the last piece of regular steam operation in the Andes will be gone for ever.

Is there any other steam in the Andes? The answer is a qualified yes. There is no longer anything with any regularity from Chile to Peru, Bolivia to Colombia, but to the intrepid explorer steam *can* be found, though only on very rare occasions where there is a failure or a problem. The G & Q is the last regular operation apart from the dock shunters at Bolivian Guaqui high up on the shores of Lake Titicaca.

The Andes give birth to the Amazon, one of whose tributaries is the Madeira River, a midwife to one of the most isolated railways in the world, the Madeira Mamore, 300 miles inland on the western borders of Brazil. It has no branch lines, makes no other railway connections and its nearest neighbouring railway is more than 700 miles distant. Today, though considerably truncated, the Madeira Mamore still runs and what is more steam is its only motive power.

The station yard at Porto Velho, terminus of the Madeira Mamore Railway, an isolated metre-gauge line in the far west of Brazil. On the left is Alco 2-8-2 No. 15 (69450/41); behind this is Baldwin No. 50 (58282/25) originally owned by the Dona Teresa Cristina Railway.

The railway has a fascinating history. Promoted as early as the 1860s but not completed until 1912, this metre-gauge line has an unenviable reputation as the 'railway of death'. It ran from Guayara Mirim on the Bolivian/Brazilian border to Porto Velho on the river Madeira, some 227 miles distant, its purpose being to link the valuable rubber production of the area with the Amazon and the coast. But the British had got into the rubber market fast and were growing rubber in Malaya, having exported seeds from Brazil by stealth. This loss plus the opening of the

Panama Canal took away virtually all the traffic. Tradition has it that each sleeper represents the loss of a human life; perhaps this is an exaggeration but there is no doubt that deaths were very high indeed – some estimates reckon that at least 6,000 workers died. Malaria was undoubtedly the biggest killer, but yellow fever must have run it a close second.

The surprise is that the railway has survived at all. It was taken over by the Brazilian government in 1937, handed over to the military in 1966 and then with Bolivia's agreement replaced in 1972 by a road, with much of its equipment dumped in the jungle or sold for scrap. Today the remains of Baldwins and box cars lie stripped of their fittings, forlorn and overgrown in the jungle alongside the tracks. The army took over the locomotive depot and works at Porto Velho and that appeared to be that: in 1979 it was proposed that any unsold and easily available assets be sold for scrap. No such thing occurred, for the announcement produced a reaction throughout the country, whose citizens made the point that the railway should be kept as

Schwartzkopff 2-8-2 No. 18 on a short train standing in the middle of the Brazilian jungle at Santo Antonio in October 1985. The Madeira Mamore Railway was driven through swamps and jungle at the end of the last century to bring valuable rubber and other commodities down to the Madeira River (a tributary of the Amazon) and thus the sea. It is said that deaths through disease, particularly malaria, were at the rate of one for every sleeper laid.

103

a memorial to those who died during its construction; others, perhaps more practical, pointed out that the new road was not an all-weather one. The outcome has been that the recently created state of Rondonia stepped in and began a programme of restoration of the line as a local amenity.

As railway preservationists in the Western world know only too well, restoring a railway is a back-breaking and expensive business, and so it has been with the Madeira Mamore. The first five miles out of Porto Velho to Santo Antonio were the worst, for here, on the edge of the town, the track had been lifted and people had built homes over the right of way. The rest of the line is virtually intact – who wants the doubtful pleasure of taking up tracks through a jungle? To date some 15½ miles out of Porto Velho to Teotonio have been reopened, as this present terminus and Santo Antonio are points on the river with spectacular rapids, providing popular tourist attractions and safe bathing for the Porto Velho townsfolk.

The locomotives and rolling stock posed a further problem, since not only had these been left out in the tropical climate uncared for over a long period but also more valuable parts, such as connecting and coupling rods as well as non-ferrous items, had been stripped and sold off. In the event it was found possible to restore an Alco 2-8-2 (69450 of 1941) and a Schwartzkopff 2-8-2 (10608 of 1936) to working order; the railway has also acquired a Baldwin small-wheeled Pacific (58282 of 1925) from the coal-carrying Dona Teresa Cristina Railway at the opposite end of the country, while four bogie coaches have also been purchased from redundant metre-gauge lines. The railway reopened on 10 July 1982.

Porto Velho can scarcely be called a metropolis but for a town in the middle of the Brazilian jungle accessible only via dirt road, river or air, it is of some size. The airport building is a tin shed, albeit a large one, where the very few visiting enthusiasts are faced (if they do not already have a

Left: Two of the huge 2-10-4 Baldwin and Alco locomotives of the Dona Teresa Cristina Railway at Tuberao in eastern Brazil in September 1977. Now virtually worn out and sadly no longer in service, these powerful machines were among the largest metre-gauge steam engines ever to work in South America.

Tuberao, the headquarters of the Dona Teresa Cristina Railway, in October 1977. In the yard are two locomotives: one of the huge Alco 2-10-4s used to work the coal trains from the mines down to the port at Imbituba, and now worn out (replaced by diesels and ex-Argentine 2-10-0s), and Baldwin Pacific No. 50 used as the 'yard goat'. The latter is now in the far west, sitting rather forlornly on the isolated metre-gauge Madeira Mamore Railway at Porto Velho.

valid certificate) with a yellow fever injection. After a suitable bargain has been struck a taxi can be found for the journey to the Madeira Mamore station, fortunately still intact; outside, landscaped gardens replace what was once the turntable and locomotive disposal area. In the yard across the tracks and adjacent to the corrugated iron 'museum' and workshop, two dead engines and one warm engine stand hopefully waiting the future: the Alco has worn its tyres so badly that they look like pulley wheels and is thus out of service, the Baldwin just waits patiently but the Schwartzkopff is in light steam in readiness for tomorrow's train, smart with silver paint on its

smokebox and with wood stacked high on the tender.

On Sundays trains to Santo Antonio run on a hourly basis – more or less – and they get very full indeed. The fare is only pence, for the service is run for the benefit of the locals, who take full advantage of it. The train, made up of the whole heterogeneous set of stock and headed by the Schwartzkopff 2-8-2, trundles through the gate to the army depot and out through the outskirts of the town, where boys throw handfuls of dirt road at the passengers for the fun of it. But this is over in a couple of minutes and then it is solid jungle all the way. Because there is no brake the speed rarely exceeds 20 mph, giving plenty of opportunity to spot the wrecked engines and box cars that litter the vegetation on either side; soon they will be completely overgrown and invisible. In 15 minutes or so the train stops at a halt-type platform while the crowd detrain, transistor radios playing, for the rapids – how they will cram themselves in for a return journey all at once is their worry! The Schwartzkopff moves off with its train a further half a mile, turns on a wye and makes its way back to Porto Velho for another load. It is the beginning of a busy day.

Brazil is also home to another

Today diesels have arrived and the Texas 2-10-4s are worn out, dumped with the now totally redundant Mallets, but steam is there in force in the form of ex-Argentine Santa Fe-type 2-10-2s put to work as their replacements. Traffic is intense as there are 18 coal-loading points in the Santa Catarina coalfield, and all that is not used at the power station at Tuberao has to be taken to the Atlantic port of Imbituba hauled by 31 locomotives using 868 wagons. The trains, taking into account their frequency and length, form a veritable torrent, delivering valuable coal to the coast for Brazil's coastal and export trade. The

As the giant 2-10-4s expired with time, new motive power was needed for the heavy coal traffic on the Dona Teresa Cristina Railway. Some diesels have now been obtained but steam is by no means dead as a number of 2-10-2s have been imported from surplus Argentina Railways' stock. These have come from the General Belgrano Railway and most are Skoda-built. This photograph was taken in October 1981.

fascinating railway, quite the opposite to the Madeira Mamore: the Dona Teresa Cristina Railway, 100 miles or so of intensive activity, is now over a century old. The railway is a coal-carrier and a big one at that, an important link in the country's energy supply train: ordinary freight and all passenger trains ceased running in 1968, improved roads making this once valuable service to the local countryside no longer viable. Until a few years ago it was entirely steam-operated using Mallets and huge 2-10-4 Texas-type locomotives, the largest rigid-framed metre-gauge engines ever and typical examples of Baldwin or Alco practice.

main workshops, and very modern ones at that, are at Tuberao: one for locomotives, another for rolling stock, a sleeper treatment shop, a permanent way workshop, plus a central office building and a social centre – quite a complex. The Dona Teresa Cristina Railway is very much a working one with no room for nostalgia; its steam is there to do a job and it does it.

South of the Brazilian border lies Paraguay, home to 231 miles of standard-gauge railway which creeps through the pampas and over swamps from the capital Asuncion to Encarnacion on the wide Parana River. Built in 1911 as the Paraguay Central, the line was laid with 60 lb rail which

Asuncion station, terminus of the Presidente Carlos Antonio Lopez Railway, a standard-gauge line which runs from the capital over the pampas to Encarnacion where there is a train ferry across the Parana River to Argentina. All locomotives are wood-fired and this ancient 2-6-0 making ready for the daily passenger train is being 'logged up' in the station yard in August 1977.

now, after three-quarters of a century, must be somewhat lighter than it was originally. The journey behind a British-built wood-burning Mogul takes 18 hours more or less, usually more. Average speed is less than 15 mph. The railway's importance stems from the link between two countries; a train ferry joins Encarnacion with Argentinian Posadas, thus opening a direct route capital to capital, Asuncion to Buenos Aires. During the first 30 years of operation the Paraguay Central did all that was expected of it, promoting economic development, particularly sugar, timber and ranching, but in 1939 American credit provided the wherewithal to construct Paraguay's only all-weather highway, parallel to the railway of course; with inevitable results. Nationalization

came in 1961 and today the railway goes under the grand name Ferrocarril Presidente Carlos Antonio Lopez (FCPCAL), after its founder. The departure of the old management led to what one writer has succinctly described as 'new blood but not new enterprise'; even a decade ago when this was written, the continued operation of the line had already acquired the aura of a daily miracle.

The terminus at Asuncion, a double-platformed affair, at least carries some charisma with its corrugated iron roof carefully hidden by wooden beams and its mosaic-tiled platform. Today it is kept very locked except at train times; it is also bisected by a new motor road. There are still trains to Buenos Aires once a week (two through coaches) with the journey taking up to three days; FCPCAL, the train ferry and Argentina Railways, all have something slightly unreal to offer. The creeping, rolling train, sometimes running on track laid directly on to the ground without the benefit of ballast, is likely to be made up of a bogie wagon of logs for fuel, two coaches, one of these a first-class chair car, and a diner whose chef cooks on a wood-burning stove. The whole open-platformed entourage, lacking vestibule connections, makes a walk through the yawing train an athletic occasion.

Most days the train leaves Asuncion near to time, crawling out of the station into the back streets, a shower of wood sparks coming from the 2-6-0's shapely chimney and dropping gently to the ground; its buffers have been hinged back – this causes less damage to straying cattle as they are swept up by the cow-catcher. Once in the countryside the rails are just visible amid the greenery. It is 60 miles to Sapucai, the first large station, which takes around four hours; the main works are here, useful if some mechanical problems have occurred on the journey. Then comes Villa Rica on the edge of the cattle country, which actually boasts two adequate hotels if you have had enough by now. After leaving town the train rolls through grasslands, with herds of steers and the occasional

cowboy alongside the track, to San Salvador (107 miles), a very adequate twin-platformed station and junction for the 35-mile-long branch to Abai. There is a shed here where engines are changed as the wood in the wagon behind the 2-6-0's tender is almost exhausted by now. Then it is a long haul south (San Salvador is not quite halfway) to Encarnacion, either in sweltering heat or pouring rain – it is one or the other in Paraguay – and the thought of a good wash plus a bed. Unless of course you are going right through, braving the ferry, with its wood-fired winding engine, for the slipway at Pacu-Cua, before the comparative comfort and speed of rail travel in Argentina.

At present there is a bridge under construction over the Parana River; rumour has it that a rail link may be open in a couple of years but there will be a road link too. The future of the FCPCAL could well be in the balance. In spite of these storm clouds further engines have been purchased from redundant Argentine stock.

At least as things are, the railway in Paraguay serves the same purpose as many railways in South America, not, as one might expect, transportation but employment. It is also cheap and as the government is competing with private road operations, it keeps charges low, with consequent overall savings to the country. In South America politics dominate the future. With all this in mind, maybe miracles will continue to happen and the FCPCAL may reach its centenary with steam.

A passenger train *en route* from Encarnacion to Paraguay's capital in October 1985. Headed by British-built 2-6-0 No. 59, the train is made up of two coaches plus a dining car (wood-fuel stove in the tiny kitchen) and a bogie wagon for extra logs.

Right: Almost unbelievably the 2 ft 0 in gauge railway from New Jalpaiguri to Darjeeling continues to operate and repeated storm damage is still repaired, dispelling rumours of imminent closure. This twisting and hilly route is worked by 0-4-0 saddle side and well tanks of ancient vintage; No. 799 is seen here just above the loop at Agony Point with the 08.50 from New Jalpaiguri to Darjeeling on 1 December 1984.

THE INDIAN SUBCONTINENT

It is breakfast time at the Windamere (sic) hotel, Darjeeling; the menu card printed on a 1930s typewriter lists 'Scotch Porridge, eggs, bacon, kidneys, toast, tea and coffee with marmalade'. The kidneys and bacon are tinned, the eggs not bad at all; the hotel's colonial style is fading a little but there are coal fires in every bedroom as well as in the comfortable lounges. Beyond the dining-room windows, on a steeply inclined pathway leading to the myriad of steps down towards the town, the beggars are lining up in order of precedence, pleased that the mist is beginning to lift. The weak sun beckons to the diners who have come to see an almost mythical railway – the Darjeeling Himalayan 2 ft gauge line climbing and twisting its way up from New Jalpaiguri. Both the Windamere and Everest hotels have hosted many an enthusiast as well as providing a near home-from-home for those visiting the hill station while on Indian service. Like so many before and after them the diners have been up at 4 a.m. in the hope of seeing the sun rise from Tiger Hill with Mount Everest illuminated in its rays. On this day nothing was visible but the prevailing mist.

The first step is to hire a taxi. There are plenty of these about in the form of battered Ambassadors – Indian-built Morris Oxfords, only even more sluggish. Settling for an elderly Land Rover long beyond passing a road-worthiness test, we set off down the ever-twisting mountain road to find the morning train coming up from the junction, hoping that it will be late, and noting the painted sign on the mountainside, 'Slow has four letters – so has life. Speed has five letters – so has death'. The driver tries for a world record for coasting downhill – not hard when it is a descent of 2,130 m (7,000 ft). As the Land Rover descends, the mist lifts a little and the railway stands out more clearly, hugging the hillside on the one hand and running

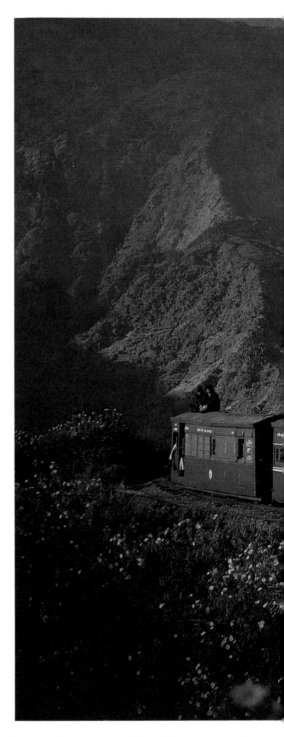

down the streets of the villages or small towns on the other. It is a good couple of hours to Sukna at the foot of the railway's mountain section, where the train from flatter Siliguri is broken up into parts for the ascent, a ride which one eminent railway author has described as a journey to Shangri-La.

Not so long ago it was possible to begin this epic journey by taking No. 43 down, the Darjeeling Mail leaving

Calcutta at 7.30 in the evening and reaching New Jalpaiguri at 8.30 next morning – and by steam at that. Now steam has gone from the Mail but the charming blue-painted Darjeeling-Himalayan class B 0-4-0 saddle side and well tanks are still on the job – acting for all the world like hill ponies struggling their way up the mountainsides, twisting, turning and looping with their 32 tons permitted load behind them. Train No. 1 up is an hour late leaving. It will be getting dark by the time it arrives at Darjeeling but the train crews are hardy, ever cheerful tribesmen; they belong to the railway and it belongs to them. Every man knows his part, from the driver to the brakeman on each carriage or wagon with intercommunication by whistle cord extending the length of the train along the roofs of the stock.

A scene on the Darjeeling-Himalayan Railway on 23 December 1980. Class B 0-4-0 saddle side and well tank No. 797 climbs into the morning sun as it takes the 07.00 from Kurseong to Darjeeling. A large part of the route is alongside the road and progress is very slow compared with the somewhat rickety but regular bus service.

For the first five miles the class B moves easily, crossing the main line to Assam at Siliguri Junction, then running down beside the road to Sukna where the train is split into its sections. The more dramatic alignments come early for all the Z reverses as well as three out of the four spirals are on the lower half of the line, although on the Darjeeling-Himalayan Railway everything is dramatic. There is a tea stop alongside the road at Tindaria (the works here are out of bounds – too near the Chinese border) and then flat out, her bunker piled high with Assam coal and with two human sanders perched on steps to the front of each cylinder, the blue B makes for Kurseong, the most important intermediate station; it is a climb of 1,460 m (4,800 ft) in 35 miles. Here the train, paying due respect to the little town's important position, backs down into the platform. This is where India ends and Central Asia begins.

Out of Kurseong after another tea stop the train runs past open fronts of shops and up through bazaar-like streets, attacking the mountain slope with barking vigour. Small boys hitch rides and jump off laughing, some trucks coming too fast down the winding roads have near misses and the odd bicycle parked too close to the track suffers disaster; it is much like any other day. The railway grade is now 1 in 25, almost continuous. The trees begin to differ, with chestnuts, willows and maples replacing the jungle growth of the Terai; prayer flags start to fly from houses and grave markers or chortens can be seen on the hillsides. The summit is at Ghum, 2,255 m (7,400 ft) and 51 miles, then, once over the top, the Himalayas proper come into view on the left with Kanchenjunga suspended in the sky at 8,598 m (28,216 ft), 50 miles away; beyond is the Chinese border. On the descent the most dramatic point is the Batasia Loop, two superimposed spirals, with the high snow-capped mountains straight ahead as the train enters and on its tail as it leaves. Then down four short miles through the deodars to the north-east frontier of India's

railways, Darjeeling, its period-piece station unaltered from the 1930s. The journey has taken almost eight hours and the train has climbed up $1\frac{1}{2}$ vertical miles in 55 horizontal ones.

Weary and almost drugged with the day's journey the enthusiast drags himself up the steps to the Windamere and collapses in a chair in the warm and comfortable lounge, a welcoming coal fire dancing in the grate opposite. If he is thirsty there is millet beer which is brewed in the tankard – it is remarkably drinkable.

But India is a land of contrasts, and below the foothills of the north lies a vast plain, hot and dusty and today very standardized in its steam power. The last decade has seen the disappearance of many of the smaller classes, though over 6,000 steam engines still exist on the three main gauges which abound: 5 ft 6 in (broad), 3 ft 3 in (metre) and mostly 2 ft 6 in (narrow).

The network stretches from the Himalayas to the southernmost tip of the subcontinent. For administrative convenience and the implementation of ever-increasing modernization, there are nine different zonal railways:

Lucknow shed on 22 November 1984 with a somewhat dusty WP class Pacific No. 7009; women remove ashes in the foreground.

Women sifting ashes at Burdwan locomotive depot on 19 December 1980. The engine in the background is a XC class Pacific, number indecipherable.

1 The Central Railway based on Bombay, which is mainly broad gauge of the former Great Indian Peninsular Railway with some narrow-gauge feeders, covering a total mileage of 5,409.

2 The Eastern Railway based on Calcutta and originating mainly from the old East Indian Railway. It is almost entirely broad gauge with a mileage of 2,381.

3 The South-Eastern Railway based like the Eastern on Calcutta and a southward continuation from the Eastern in the direction of Madras and the centre of the country; formerly the Bengal Nagpur Railway. Of its total length of 3,495 miles, about a third is narrow gauge.

4 The Southern Railway, which has its headquarters at Madras and takes in the whole of the southern tip of India. Its total distance is 6,162 miles, of which over two-thirds is metre gauge.

5 The South Central Railway based at Secunderabad, formerly most of the Nizam's State Railway and a large part of the Madras & Southern Mahratta Railway. It is mainly metre gauge with sections being regauged to 5 ft 6 in.

6 The Western Railway, with headquarters at Bombay. It is largely metre and narrow gauge with the broad-gauge main lines of the old Bombay Baroda and Central India to Baroda, Ahmedabad and Agra. Of the total length of 6,064 miles, all but 1,636 are metre gauge or narrow.

7 The Northern Railway based on Delhi, with lines in the Ganges Valley and Allahabad continuing to Amritsar and the Pakistan border; formerly part of the North-Western Railway with a considerable metre-gauge network south of Delhi. Its total mileage is 6,429, of which about a third is metre gauge or narrower.

8 The North-Eastern Railway based on Gorakhpur, a smaller, more isolated system covering the frontier areas along the borders of Nepal. The total mileage is just over 3,000, including metre and broad gauge.

9 The North-East Frontier Railway based at Gauhati, the capital of Assam, and serving the most eastern extremity of India known as Assam. It is formed from the metre-gauge Assam-Bengal Railway and part of the East Bengal Railway, and in more recent times a broad-gauge line connecting Gauhati with the main body of Indian Railways via New Jalpaiguri has been opened. This region is responsible for the famous 2 ft gauge line to Darjeeling.

All these railways operate some steam, though today, as has been stated earlier, this is becoming very standardized; both dieselization and electrification are moving apace. During the Second World War the United States saw to it that quantities of broad and metre gauge 2-8-2s were sent to India, their rugged characteristics standing up well to conditions there. In fact success led to success, for Baldwins received the order for the first batch of a new standard range of locomotives, the WP Pacifics. Later batches of these, built in many countries, brought the total number in the class to 775 but this was eclipsed by the WG 2-8-2 which reached as many as 2,450. These were accompanied by the smaller WL 4-6-2s as well as corresponding designs for the metre gauge, a YP Pacific, a YG 2-8-2 and YL 2-6-2. The YP Pacifics have the distinction of being the last steam express passenger engines to be built in the world, the first batches emanating from the North British Locomotives works in Glasgow and from Krauss-Maffei of Munich. The remainder were constructed in India by the Tata Engineering & Locomotive Co. of Jamshedpur. Most of today's steam is made up from these post-war designs, many of which have been built in India at the Chittaranjan Locomotive

With a polished star on its smokebox door and silvered boiler bands, WP Pacific No. 7418 leaves Kasaragod with the 06.20 Janata express from Mangalore to Hazrat Nizamuddin (Delhi) on 30 December 1980. WP Pacifics are the principal express passenger engines on India's railways, a huge class running to 775 locomotives.

Right: Cattle continue to graze at Ajmer Junction, unmoved by the departure of train number 69 up, the 16.15 to Kacheguda on 11 February 1987. The exhaust from YP class Pacific No. 2495, belonging to India's Western Railway, partially obscures the classic signal gantry guarding the south end of the station. The locomotive depot is just visible behind the wall in the background.

Opposite: With a full train-load of passengers ND class 4-6-4 No. 755 heads a 2 ft 0 in gauge local out of Bamgourgaon on 3 November 1981. The train is the 06.20 mixed from Sabalgarh to Gwalior.

Right: One of India's standard types, YG 3418, works hard as it heads a heavy west-bound freight out of Agra, Idgah, on the evening of 19 November 1984.

Works set up in 1950 with U.K. help, giving self-sufficiency in locomotive construction. Not that locomotive construction was new to India, for even in the days of the Raj a number of the old companies built their own engines, the most well-known being Bombay Baroda and Central India Railway designs constructed at Ajmer.

Today some 14 per cent of India's broad-gauge network is electrified and this work is progressing month by month; such passenger steam as is working regularly comprises only the standard classes of 4-6-2 and 2-8-2 in both broad and metre gauge services.

Left: The smallest engine at work on Indian State Railways, CS class No. 775; a 2-4-0 tank heads the 12.10 2 ft 6 in gauge train from Shantipur to Nabadwip Ghat at a wayside halt on 12 November 1981.

That is not to say that steam in India is dying – far from it – but the Mecca of dozens of different types and classes has faded into the horizon in recent years. Delhi, Lucknow, Agra, New Jalpaiguri, Mysore, Bangalore, Hyderabad, all have a great deal of steam compared with, say, Europe but little in comparison with a decade ago in India. In fact the numbers of broad-gauge steam engines still in service are now less than the total construction figure for the WP and WG classes, while the metre-gauge numbers must be just over the total of YP, YL and YG total production. The narrow gauge has also been thinned, particularly in the number of types and classes available; inevitable closures have not helped, for example, the last of the well-known Martins Light Railways, the Futwah-Islampur Light Railway, was taken over by the State and closed on 1 February 1987. In spite of all this India can still boast over 6,000 working steam locomotives even if most of them are of six standard classes.

Above: NM class 4-6-2 No. 762 heads the 15.25 Gwalior to Sabalgarh mixed out of Bamgourgaon on 3 November 1981. Note the passengers riding in the cheapest possible way on the roofs of the coaches. Contrary to South American practice, there are no foot boards and only difficult access to the box cars on the front of the train.

Steam, camels and people at Bari on 19 November 1985. The engine is 2 ft 6 in gauge Kerr Stuart 1921-built ZA/3 class 2-8-4 tank No. 735, and the train the 09.15 mixed from Dhaulpur to Tantpur.

Above: 1987 saw the demise of an historic Indian Railways' landmark when the last trains ran on the surviving Martins Light Railway, the Futwah-Islampur, a 2 ft 6 in gauge line just east of Patna. Here 0-6-2 tank No. 4H (Manning Wardle 2031/23) hauls a special train near Islampur on 25 November 1984.

Her neighbour Pakistan is still a steam paradise, though here too dieselization is proceeding apace. The great attraction in Pakistan is that a variety of old types and classes remain, including some designs produced by the British Engineering Standards Association (BESA) in 1903, a tribute to their sound design. There are three track widths, as in India, but unlike that country the metre gauge is thin on the ground – in fact there is only one system based on Mirpur Khas using M and SP class 4-6-0s and YD 2-8-2s, mostly the latter. Without doubt the star attractions on the broad gauge are the inside cylinder 4-4-0 of class SPS, mainly built by Beyer Peacock of Manchester from 1904 onwards and based at Malakwal along with the

numerically larger class SG 0-6-0 of the same period. For many years the SGS used to work the Peshawar Khyber Pass line to Landi Kotal, one engine leading, one banking. It was a Fridays only experience which tended to be suspended during military operations against local tribes and now with the Afghan problems thought to be permanently suspended or out of bounds to visiting tourists. One intrepid enthusiast once made the trip on the locomotive, being forbidden to travel in the train itself for 'safety reasons'. Riding 'point' on the buffer beam (and hanging on tight to the handrails) of the leading engine, two men kept sharp eyes on the rails ahead to ensure none of them had been removed by 'enterprising' tribesmen.

Above: The only inside cylinder 4-4-0s to survive in regular service today work over the 5 ft 6 in gauge system in Pakistan. These mainly Beyer Peacock-built beauties are based at Malakwal and are designated class SPS. Here No. 3008 leaves Malakwal on 29 March 1987 with No. 216 down, the 10.55 Lalamusa to Faisalabad passenger train.

Left: A water train leaving Kotri Junction towards Dadu behind HGS class 2-8-0 No. 2216 on 4 April 1987. These very British-outlined engines had by then been restricted mainly to shunting duties in the Hyderabad area.

Then there is the narrow gauge, always worth a visit anywhere in the world, for the slim tracks penetrate areas where few travel and the tourist is non-existent. In Pakistan this is very much the case and there is one journey which is a must. Long and difficult, it involves a visit to Quetta, a hill station for the soldiers of the Raj, then over the 184-mile-long 2 ft 6 in gauge line from Bostan to Zhob (Fort Sandeman) with its desert-like route interspersed with stretches of country of unbeliev-

Another scene at Malakwal, showing a further example of standard British locomotive practice, the inside cylinder 0-6-0: on 30 March 1987 SGS No. 2510 leaves Malakwal with train No. 470 down, the 11.20 passenger to Dandot. Like their sisters the SPS 4-4-0s, these SGS 0-6-0s belonged to the North-Western of India in pre-partition days; they were also regular engines for use over the always dangerous Khyber Pass line.

Opposite top: Pushing a tank car full of extra water, class SGS 0-6-0 No. 2508 climbs from Khewra to Dandot on 31 March 1987. Although Pakistan Railways are rapidly dieselizing, their elderly 0-6-0s still perform useful services on secondary lines and have survived the decimation of their larger sisters used on the faster long-distance trains.

Opposite bottom: Most services on the metre-gauge lines in Pakistan are now worked by the standard YD class 2-8-2s, though these SP 4-6-0s are still available. On 23 March 1987 SP 141 was working train number MG25, the morning mixed from Nawabshah to Mirpur Khas, at Shafiabad.

able greens against a backdrop of snow-capped peaks for most of the year. It runs parallel with the Afghan border for much of its length, but its *raison d'être* was surprisingly not military but commercial – to bring valuable chrome to the factories of old India and, even more important, Great Britain. The line has been a victim of Soviet-funded tribesmen in recent times but trains still run irregularly and the journey is one of the most remote on the Indian subcontinent. The railway is worked

by class G 2-8-2s but timekeeping and days of operation can be very erratic for obvious reasons. The whole Quetta Division has suffered from disturbed conditions in the area but at the time of writing, matters are improving some-what, an encouraging sign.

South, beyond the tip of India, is Sri Lanka, which still uses steam on its narrow-gauge line out of Colombo but today pride of place must go to the enterprising venture entitled the Vice-roy Special, a steam tourist train using

restored 4-6-0 tender tank engines as well as the more conventional Armstrong Whitworth 4-6-0s. Steam never died completely in Sri Lanka because a number of these old stalwarts were lying waiting in sheds in various places in the south and central areas, particularly at Kandy and Colombo. Fortunately the shed master at Colombo was always a steam enthusiast and although engines in his custody may not have felt well, they were seldom allowed to die. Recent troubles on the island cannot have helped this operation but let us hope that, in Sri Lankan tradition, steam is only taking an afternoon nap and not a permanent sleep.

Perhaps the final word about the Indian subcontinent should go to the Indian railway authorities and the tourist industry, who have introduced a novel partially steam-hauled train which appeals to railway lovers and tourists alike – the Palace on Wheels. Among the many splendid sights encountered in India are the magnificently opulent palaces of the great Maharajas who ruled and lived in (to say the least) a grand and elegant manner. As might be expected, when these near-gods travelled, they did so in a manner to which they were accustomed. For their journeys by rail, each ruler commissioned his own royal train – a veritable palace on wheels similar to but more ornate than that of our own royal family – which enabled the Maharaja to move around in style in a vehicle or vehicles which were in effect an extension of his own home. Many of these splendid coaches have been retained and the authorities have now put together a metre-gauge train of 13 of them, dating from 1890 to 1930. The traveller is taken back in time on a visit by rail to Rajastan from Delhi, travelling to Jaipur, Udaipur, Jaisalmer and Jodhpur, and back via Bharatpur and Agra. Four days of this trip are guaranteed to be steam-hauled, giving an attractive package in considerable comfort to those who can afford those extra few pounds – or maybe dollars. It is an enterprising venture which deserves success.

Left: A line which has suffered considerable problems in the Russo-Afghan war is the Bostan to Zhob (Fort Sandeman) narrow-gauge railway in Pakistan. Running adjacent to the border it has been blown up on several occasions but after a year and a half of inactivity the first train to travel the entire length of the line is seen here leaving Khanai on 28 November 1986 using two 2-8-2s, No. 6SGS in the front and No. 46G banking.

Three photographs showing scenes on the 2 ft 6 in gauge Nepal Janakpur Railway on 29 November 1984. *Opposite top*: 0-6-2 tank *Surya* (Hunslet 3875/62) leaves Khajuri with a train from Jaynagar to Janakpurdam. *Opposite bottom*: The railways' sole operational Garratt (now only used for special enthusiast parties) 2-6-2 + 2-6-2 No. 6 *Sitarram* on a bridge between Khajuri and Jaynagar near the border with India. *Left*: The amazing partly open-air workshops at Khajuri with the Garratt just visible on the right.

Left: Very little steam moves in Burma today though shortages of diesel fuel bring various classes, including YB Pacifics and YD 2-8-2s, back into service on passenger trains. There are even some Garratts still stored at Thazi. This metre-gauge system was using steam more regularly on 1 December 1975 when YB class 2-8-2 No. 539 worked the 07.05 Mandalay to Madaya service; it is seen here coming into Mandalay Fort.

129

Right: Some of China's now elderly and extremely interesting steam locomotives can be found at work in industry. Here at the Baotou Steel Company American-built (1920) 0-8-0 tank No. ET1 5342 and 2-6-0 No. 179 were hard at work in 1981. The flagman on No. 179 is in fact a flagwoman.

Below: A QJ class 2-10-2 takes a heavy freight over the Hongshui River near Harbin station on the line from Changsha to Guilin in southern China. Passenger services on this route are now diesel but QJs continue to work much of the freight, having replaced the old Russian FD class 2-10-2 which now lie rusting at the back of the motive power depots waiting for scrapping.

CHINA

As dawn breaks and the sun's rays clear the mountain peaks, snow-capped even in summer, two huge 2-10-2 steam engines pound the grades from the westernmost end of China's Great Wall on the borders of the Gobi Desert and head for Lanzhou on the Silk Road. Over 1,600 kilometres away and more, as the crow flies, the same sun heralds the beginning of another day at Manzhouli on the Russian border, where a spotless 2-8-2, its brasswork polished, boiler bands gleaming and chimney ringed with shining brass, begins its ten-minute run into Soviet territory with the once weekly through train from Beijing to Moscow. In Harbin, Changchun, Jilin, Shenyang and points north, Manchurian steam-depots coal, water and generally service steam engines that run into well over four figures and comprise modern 2-10-2s, old and new 2-8-2s, two classes of Pacific; the variety is not great but the numbers are. Further south steam is no longer present in the abundance of the 1970s but there are further thousands of 2-10-2s and 2-8-2s at work on freights and in the marshalling yards, with Pacifics on some cross-country services. True, the great new lines driving through the western mountains and those of the far south have either lost their steam or have never seen it, though this scarcely lessens their fascination. China's railways are on the march.

Right top: No. 09, one of the standard 0-8-0 steam locomotives used on China's 760 mm gauge railways, local or forestry, waits at the terminus of the Sanhetun Forestry Railway in Jilin Province to pick up empty timber bolster wagons in October 1986. No. 09 was built at Shiziazhang in central China but these powerful little engines were built as far away as Finland and Hungary as well as in China (still under construction today) and have small variations in design.

Although China welcomes an interest in her railways and even goes out of her way to arrange tours for interested groups, the authorities find it difficult to understand the Westerner's enthusiasm for steam: to them the railway is a functional organization, China's principal means of mass transportation, with modernization and increased efficiency quite rightly taking priority. This does not mean that they have no use for steam – far from it. East-north-east of Beijing the smog-bound industrial city of Datong is unique in today's world: it produces five *new*, brand new, mainline steam locomotives a week.

A visit to Datong Steam Locomotive Factory is a journey into the past. It also shows a Chinese ability to exploit two of the country's main assets, vast quantities of cheap coal and labour. The factory, like most other large industrial organizations in China, is a 'cradle to grave' affair, a whole city within itself, with houses, schools, crèches, recreation facilities, technical colleges, hospitals; paternalism and the direction of labour ensure that the 8,700 workforce is on the job daily. There are 23 workshops, from foundry to steam test, from raw materials to the finished product – either a 2-10-2 QJ class or a 2-8-2 JS class. To those who remember the past glories of say Crewe in England, Baldwins in the U.S.A. or Henschel in Germany, a visit is full of nostalgia: frames on great planing machines, heavy cylinder castings, wheel sets all gleaming and painted, the continual rattle of the boiler shop and the thrill of the final erecting shop. Visitors often get a ride on 'tomorrow's engine', a QJ or JS on final test.

Today Datong is looking to the future with the design of fully modernized steam engines in mind. David Wardale, whose forward thinking brought South Africa's steam to such a height of efficiency, has been two years at Datong as a consultant; the Chinese are always happy to learn, though politics may well ensure that there is no real long-term future for steam even here.

In strict truth Datong is not quite unique as there is one other factory turning out steam engines – Tangshan works makes the small SY class 2-8-2, mostly used for yard or industrial purposes. It probably produces 100 engines a year – indeed it has only just got back into its stride after the disastrous earthquake of 1976.

Although the vast majority of steam locomotives work over the standard-gauge tracks of the national network, they can also be found in some abundance on two other types of railway, the busy non-stop industrial lines and some narrow-gauge systems. The use of steam traction in heavy industry is considerable, especially in the giant steelworks as far apart as Anshan in Manchuria and Wuhan in the south, or, for example, in the vast open-cast coal-mining area of Fushun near Shenyang. Industry provides a greater variety of older classes, 2-6-0s, 2-6-2s, 2-8-0s, 2-8-2s, and 0-6-0 tanks.

The narrow-gauge lines can be divided into three types: isolated systems of 760 mm local railways, many of which have now gone diesel; long forestry railways in the timber-studded north-east (29 out of the country's 76 of these are in Jilin Province); and the French-built metre-gauge line extending up from the Vietnamese border (once French Indo-China) to Kunming in the south-west – China's City of Eternal Spring. The local railways and the forestry lines are very standardized, using 0-8-0s built in Finland (reparations to Russia), Russia, Poland, Hungary and, today, China.

The metre gauge in the south-west is virtually 100 per cent diesel; modernization took place in parallel with the construction of the Chinese-built (also metre-gauge) Tan-Zam Railway linking landlocked Zambia with the Indian Ocean at Dar Es Salaam in Tanzania a decade and more ago – the motive power is the same. Because of this system's proximity to the still un-settled border regions, most of it is out of bounds to foreigners, certainly the part south of Yi Liang some four hours beyond Kunming.

Left bottom: Datong steam locomotive works in north-east China still turns out between 250 and 300 locomotives every year. Two classes are at present under construction, the JS 2-8-2 replacing the older JF of the same wheel arrangement, and the huge QJ 2-10-2. This scene in the erecting shop photographed in November 1987 shows a JS in the final stages of erection prior to steam testing.

Taiyuan shed on the line south from Kunming to the Vietnamese border: in the foreground, used as a stationary boiler, is a French JF51 class 2-8-2 tank once belonging to the Chemin de Fer de Yunan, while in the background are two KD55 2-8-2s, the standard steam engine class introduced by the Japanese and principal motive power over this hilly route until the coming of the diesels in the 1970s.

Unfortunately Western eyes are not likely to see it before what appears to be imminent closure. The Chinese railway authorities confirmed to the author in 1987 that the line was still working on an 'infrequent' basis.

Many of the railways belonging to the Forestry Bureau extend up to 160 kilometres into the woodlands (some even have a number of branch lines) and handle hundreds of thousands of cubic metres of timber each year. The gauge has been measured at 762 mm or exactly 2 ft 6 in. Some of these lines date back to the Japanese occupation but many appear to have been built almost immediately after 'Liberation', that is, 1949, when a substantial amount of railway-oriented aid was provided by the Soviet Union. This would certainly account for the loco-motives built in Finland, Poland, Russia and Hungary. All these railways need permits either from the Forestry Bureau or the Public Security Bureau or both. Each runs a passenger service using miniature versions of Chinese National Railways' slatted-seated hard-class coaches painted in the familiar green with yellow stripes; these trains tend to run in the hours of darkness and are basically 'workmen's trains'.

The last decade has seen a consider-able clearing out of non-Chinese-built non-standard classes, which is hardly surprising when one considers the advent of 250 new steam engines a year from Datong and the introduction of diesel power for virtually all long-distance express passenger services bar a few in the north-west or north-east. Not that this has been unwelcome to the traveller, for diesels have obviated locomotive changes and speeded up services; the same applies to the continuing electrification programme. Apart from the JF6 class 2-8-2, the American-built Baldwin or Alco 2-8-0 KD7 (mostly on yard duties in the Shanghai area and around Nanchang), it is difficult to think of any foreign-built steam still at work on the National system, even though steam abounds in industry and on some narrow-gauge local railways. Even the giant Russian-built FD class 2-10-2s

At the time of writing a very small amount of steam survives in the form of French-built JF 51 class 2-8-2 tanks for trip working and the odd Japanese KD55 class 2-8-0 steamed for yard work, but all this is in forbidden territory. Until 1986 there were a number of KD55s dead at Kunming Bei yard but these, bar one (said to be preserved), have now been cut up. One gem remains in Yunnan – just – a 600 mm gauge all-steam line branching off the metre-gauge system at Jijie; this twisting mountainous piece of railway, when it works, uses 1924 ex-Baldwin 0-10-0s over its 34-km length to Gejiu.

One of China's most modern locomotive classes, QJ 2-10-2 No. 901, breasts the summit of the steep grades up the Nankou Pass and approaches Qinglongqiao (new) station in October 1984. Autumn colours are just appearing and the Great Wall of China is visible directly above the locomotive. A further QJ is at the rear of the train acting as a banker but Qinglongqiao station is a terminus on a reverse, thus No. 901 will leave as a banker, returning light after reaching Badalang station, the next stop.

have gone to their last rest as they have been remorselessly displaced by the indigenous QJ. However, at best the Soviet engines were second-hand regauged locomotives, which filled a much needed gap while Chinese production got into swing. Up until about 1985 it was not hard to find foreign-built relics lying dumped in sheds and locomotive repair works (Japanese conjugated valve gear 2-8-2s, Japanese 2-6-4 tanks, Japanese and British-built Pacifics, Alco 2-6-2 tanks and even a British 1907 2-6-2 saddle tank) but the edict went out to break them up, and that was that. Maybe there were too many foreign groups anxious to look into corners.

135

Right: One of China's three named locomotives and the only steam locomotive thus treated (replacing an older JF), *Marshall Zhu-de* awaits his next turn of duty at Harbin shed in October 1984. The engine carries a polished brass plaque of the Marshall on the smokebox door, as well as brass boiler bands and a further plaque on the cab sides.

Before the Second World War the Western powers had brought considerable influence to bear on Chinese railways and locomotives, many being built and worked by them. For example, the Kowloon-Canton Railway was British while the South Manchurian Railway had considerable American influence after regauging from the Russian system – even when it was taken over and run by the Japanese. The Manchurian lines were certainly modernized by the Japanese during their tenure, with fast and extremely luxurious expresses running

Above: The scrapyard at Lanzhou locomotive repair factory in north-west China in October 1984. Standing forlornly awaiting its fate is a North British Locomotive Company 2-6-2 saddle tank, thought to be class PL5 No. 70, dating from 1907. It had been out of use for a decade and was cut up in 1986.

from the principal cities to the coast; one of the streamlined Pacifics is still in working order at Shenyang Railway Museum. Also, as mentioned earlier, Japanese steam penetrated the metre-gauge lines south of Kunming where the KD55 2-8-0 became the major unit of steam power.

One of the better-known foreign engines to serve in China in its day was the 1935 Vulcan Foundry-built KF1 4-8-2, designed by Col. Kenneth Cantlie for the Canton-Hankou and Shanghai-Nanking railways. An extremely modern and efficient machine, an example has been donated and shipped back to England, where it now resides in the National Railway Museum at York.

Modern steam in China is efficiently run and well cared for, each large

region having its own locomotive repair factory and each sizeable depot its repair facilities, engines going to the main works generally on a mileage-run basis. Harbin depot, for example, houses around 80 to 100 locomotives, according to seasonal work; they comprise QJ 2-10-2s along with JS and JF 2-8-2s, with visiting SL Pacifics from nearby secondary lines. Like Western sheds capable of undertaking intermediate repairs, the depot can handle wheel-turning and boiler-tube replacements as well as periodical cylinder and valve examinations. During the course of a single day the shed would expect to coal and water 200 or so locomotives including Harbin's own special QJ, *Marshall Zhu-de*, one of China's three named locomotives. Each locomotive is likely to have its

Left: One of the earlier QJ class 2-10-0s, No. 1002 (Mudanjang works 1958), in use as a wash-out engine on Harbin shed during October 1984. Harbin depot is a standard American pattern semi-roundhouse with a repair works attached, and housed, at the time, QJ, JF and JS classes as well as servicing visiting SL Pacifics.

Right: Two classes of Chinese steam locomotives at work in Harbin freight yard in the early 1980s. On the left is the yard pilot, a JF 2-8-2; in the centre is a QJ 2-10-2 and to the right is another JF fly shunting. Harbin is a collecting point for prodigious loads of timber coming in from the forests of the north-east.

own permanent crews (driver, assistant driver and fireman), three crews per locomotive allowing it to perform at as high a mileage as possible but returning to depot once the divisional boundary, probably 200 kilometres, has been reached. Some crews go into the locomotive repair factories with their engine, as they did in France. But times are beginning to change and the 'common user' policy operated in Great Britain could well be making headway – certainly in late 1987 this was being tried in some areas, with resulting dirty locomotives.

The observer is likely to see more and more QJs taking over where once RM Pacifics or JFs were common-place; local passenger trains and hump yards are examples. Strangely the older SL Pacifics based on an earlier Japanese design appear to have a better chance of remaining in service, at least for a while, than the later built RM. Until very recent years the RMs could be seen regularly on the longer secondary routes but now diesels have taken over most workings except on those lines in the north-east where it is cold, very cold, in winter. Jilin shed in the heartland of Manchuria, east of the provincial capital of Changchun and half a day's journey over the single line from Shengyang, still houses a number of SL Pacifics. They work the local services to Changchun as well as the 300-km journey to Tong hua south-east of the city. Until 1986 this class also headed trains northwards over the tracks leading to Harbin. The shed at Jilin is an ex-South Manchurian Railway semi-roundhouse, as yet unrebuilt and thus a rarity. It presently houses not only SL Pacifics but also JF 2-8-2s and the ubiquitous QJs, though on occasions an RM comes in from Changchun, a situation which will not last as these passenger trains are about to go diesel.

One Changchun train leaves Jilin in the early morning and at first light it is hard to discern just what is on the head end – as one emerges from the ticket barrier on the platform there is no time to go forward to look: there is a seat to find and platform access is only

allowed shortly before departure. There are two classes of travel to choose from as this is not an express but a 'fast train' with hard-sitting or soft-sitting coaches. Hard-sitting is basic, sometimes very basic; soft-sitting in this case is a single composite coach at the rear of the train, an American-type chair-car with loose covered seats, antimacassars for your head and mugs on the window shelves ready for the boiling water brought round by the coach attendant, who will also provide packets of green tea for a few fen. Next to the composite is the diner and as the train is off the tourist route and a local, breakfast is likely to be rice, noodles and some vegetables. If the chef is enterprising and the foreigner prepared to wait, the Chinese version of a tasty Western breakfast may well be produced – maize bread dipped in egg and fried, then put together as a jam sandwich and re-fried – served very hot and to be eaten with chopsticks. On a Manchurian winter's morning, this can be very good indeed.

It is only a short journey (in Chinese terms) before reaching industrial Changchun, already smog-bound as the factory chimneys begin their daily stint. Changchun is very much a railway town, with a steam locomotive repair factory, a large depot and one of China's major carriage works. In addition, for the inter-urban fans there is an interesting tramway system that still uses some old wooden-bodied cars. As the train runs in, on the right-hand side the observer can see track upon track of fully occupied sidings, spread out from the neck of the hump yard just to the north of the station platform, the hump engine a JF 2-8-2 or maybe today a QJ. As the freight trains are made up, they pound out of the yard sometimes double-headed by QJs with over 2,000 tons of timber, mineral produce or livestock behind their tenders; what is more they move out every 10 to 15 minutes. This is not at all unusual, for most of China's big yards are humps, reminiscent of the days when freight traffic moved in quantity in Western Europe and the U.S.A. The

Pacific unhooks and moves off down to the shed where it is coaled, watered and turned ready for the return trip. Just another normal morning.

North from Jilin, the Harbin line splits off at the junction beyond Dragon Pond Hill, and some two hours' distant by local train the Forestry Bureau's narrow-gauge tracks meet their wider brothers for the transhipment of logs. Here, if you are lucky, you will find real Chinese hospitality for few if any foreigners come to the village or the railway. Down the dirt road, past wooden houses, chickens, dogs and horses, street stalls and shops, is the Bureau's hotel where the food is good, the colourless grain-spirit like rocket fuel, the toilet a wooden trough and a bucket, and the hospitality out of this world. You see the railway through a faint haze. Beyond the hotel is the yard where train upon train of logs arrive ready for distribution and a Hungarian-built 0-8-0 shunts fussily. There is also a loco shed and works, housing, servicing and repairing the line's steam locomotives. As it is impossible to arrive at the Forestry Bureau until late in the morning, the narrow-gauge passenger train is long gone but if you are lucky there could be a ride in a railcar going part of the way, taking staff or railway officers. This is very much a 'proper' railway using

Some 40 km away from the terminus at Sanhetun and into the beginning of the forests, 760 mm MAV (Hungarian)-built 0-8-0 No. 06 waits to collect its wagons after passing the passenger railcar (just visible to the rear) full of railway officials. Most of the local population have probably never been as far as the nearest big city of Jilin – three hours away on the main line – and the appearance of a long-nosed foreigner taking photographs was a big occasion.

single-line tokens with their appropriate loops and electric tablet instruments. At each loop there is a train, either empty cars returning to the forests or load upon load of logs on four-wheeled all-steel bolsters operated American fashion, close-coupled when empty but connected in pairs by the logs themselves when loaded, though there are a number of bogie flat wagons too. Each train has its own caboose-like brake van. By now the crisp cold air has counteracted the hospitality alcohol so the visitor begins to take in the scale of it all – and this is only one of many.

For big steam passenger working one needs to go north-east of Harbin into the cold forest lands or 27 hours west

of Datong to Lanzhou (steam all the way in 1987) and thence into the mountains which lead to Tibet or beyond the Great Wall's end. Lanzhou is a big junction, once an important point on the old Silk Road and not having lost its status today. Here lines run south, electrified, to Baoji and on to Beijing via Xian with its clay soldiers once defenders of an Emperor's tomb; west to Xining and on over the mountains to Golmod on the proposed route to Lhasa or the long, long haul to Urumqi over more mountains and through the desert lands. For all this there is a steam locomotive factory, a modern shed dealing with steam and electric power and, at the end of the station platforms, a steam

servicing point for coaling and watering QJs in from Xining, Jiayuguan or on the Datong road.

Train No. 143 leaves Lanzhou at 11.35 in the morning, arriving at Urumqi at 07.56 just under two days later; for almost a day it is steam-hauled and part of the time double-headed – one of the last great steam journeys of the world. It is not just a local but a through train. Chinese trains run in numbered blocks in the timetable, indicating their speed, and therefore their cost, per kilometre, and this one is marked FT (Fast Train), a lower category than express and thus slightly cheaper. It probably loads up to 15 cars: hard-sitting, hard-lying, a diner and one soft-lying (four-berth

QJ class 2-10-2 No. 114 stands alongside SL Pacific No. 618 at Changchun locomotive shed in November 1987. Both engines are 'foreigners', having come to the depot for servicing that morning, and are now watered and coaled. The QJ is for a heavy south-bound freight and the SL, after turning, will take the morning semi-fast to Jilin, which is its home base. By 1987 most passenger trains had been dieselized but a few Jilin turns were still Pacific worked.

A train headed by two QJ 2-10-2s climbs up into the mountains *en route* to Lanzhou from Urumqi. This is a through train to Shanghai, taking five days for the journey and passing through as many as seven provinces.

sleeper) with a couple of baggage cars. The engine for the first leg of the journey is a single QJ 2-10-2 from Lanzhou shed; a painted brass-cast red flag is fixed to the cab sides denoting that there is a prize crew on the job. These exemplary workers will quite likely fire the locomotive by hand, not using the automatic stoker and thus saving fuel. It is just on 40 minutes to Hekounan, only 42 kilometres, which shows the nature of the terrain; here the Xining (and perhaps Lhasa) line continues westwards while our train turns north to cross the Yellow River to the first divisional point, Dachaigou, where engines are changed during the 12-minute stop: 16.26 to 16.38.

From here on it is double-headed QJs for the run to Weiweinan, the line climbing steeply for the next 100 kilometres, with superb views of the hard-working engines from the train snaking behind them. It is dark before the summit but on a crisp night the ride is all the more thrilling for that, the exhaust beats clearly audible through the twice-glazed windows – even if you cannot get them open; if you do, it is smuts and black bedding all the way. As the moon rises it casts shadows and pools of inky blackness across the

valley where the line winds back and forth against the distant backdrop of snow-capped mountains. Weiweinan has another 11-minute locomotive stop when the pilot engine comes off the train and QJ remains at the head end – solo for the long run ahead. This is the time to climb into bed, dropping off to sleep as the train moves on through the night towards the desert lands and Jiayuguan, where the Great

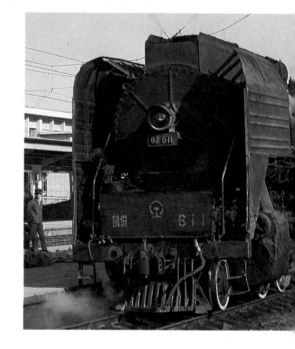

Wall has its westernmost fort. The Wall is just visible from the train across the sands; peaks rise even higher than before – seemingly impenetrable – there was no need for further fortification here.

Steam finishes at Yumen at 08.42 and the diesels come on for the next long leg; it has been the run of a modern lifetime. Yet the return trip from Jiayuguan is even better, preferably by train 51, a through Urumqi to Shanghai express (travelling a staggering distance through seven Chinese provinces), for this train makes the climb through the high mountains in full daylight next morning. As it was once in Canada and the U.S.A. – and even more recently in Soviet Russia – one can wake up in the morning to hear real steam working hard, the sound of the two exhausts reverberating back as the QJs hit the grades ahead. It is almost a window on the past.

In the clear cold air of morning, the two QJ 2-10-2s can be clearly seen out of the coach windows as they round the curves, the long train behind them twisting in the hillside; while on the opposite side of the valley the line is still hugging the rocks, a feather of steam coming from the chimney of a descending QJ. In the early sun it is an enthralling sight and an even more evocative sound – a lingering survivor

of one of the great main line steam journeys in today's world.

A change at Lanzhou can produce yet more steam – four-and-a-half hours west along the river valley to Xining (almost certainly behind a QJ from that shed) or the desert route east to Datong. Each journey has its attraction. Xining, capital city of Qinghai Province, lies in the foothills which eventually lead to Tibet and here one comes across these 'minority' people for the first time, while onwards for 20 hours the now diesel-hauled (DF4) train makes its way to 3,050 m- (10,000 ft-) high Golmod every other day, carrying a doctor as a member of staff to deal with altitude sickness. The Datong road too can be dramatic, providing the far from common experience of 27 hours of steam as the single QJ turns and twists its way into the desert hills up to a sandy summit before the spectacular descent to Zongwei. So far this route is solely steam with double-headed freights waiting in most loops but its time is running out as new DF4 diesels come off the production lines daily. China's railways are moving on very rapidly.

Above: One of the longest train journeys in China is that from Xining through to Shanghai, a five-day, seven-province trip. This is the 18.29 train headed by QJ 2-10-2 No. 912 ex-Xining shed, which will work as far as Lanzhou.

Left: Lanzhou station in November 1987 with QJ class 2-10-2 No. 611 on the afternoon train for Xining in the Tibetan foothills. Beyond here and on to Golmod lies the proposed route to Lhasa, though the line is stuck at Golmod awaiting the resolving of technical problems posed by the increasingly mountainous terrain.

143

CHAPTER 3

THE TOURIST LINES

Preceding page: Fenchurch and Stepney return from Horsted Keynes heading the Poppy Day Special on 26 October 1986, and pass under the bridge near the summit of Freshfield Bank on the Bluebell Railway in Sussex.

Below: The 1866-built 0-4-0 well tank Dolgoch at Rhyd-yr-onnen in 1951, the year the Talyllyn Railway was acquired by the Talyllyn Railway Preservation Society, the first of its kind in the world and precursor of today's worldwide steam tourist railway operations. At that time the Talyllyn was an anachronism, untouched by 85 years of trundling trains up and down the valley of the Afon Fathew.

GREAT BRITAIN

Almost at the midway point of the great arc which bounds the shores of Cardigan Bay a narrow-gauge railway, its train laden with summer tourists, wends its way up the shadowed valley from holidaymakers' Tywyn, once a modest watering hole for middle-class Victorians, to the slate village, almost a hamlet, of Abergynolwyn, some six and a half miles to the east; then round sharp curves to Nant Gwernol ravine, which is almost nowhere. The journey takes just under an hour but the passengers don't care – they have come for the fun of the ride. Even today time moves less perceptibly here and memories are longer. But old men speak no more of the Talyllyn Railway's coming, nor do nonagenarians remember the first train as though it were

yesterday. Stupendous changes have taken place since *Dolgoch*'s shrill whistle first awoke the echoes in the mountains when the Crimean War was a recent memory and the age of Victoria had reached that point where all but a few believed that there would be no end to the growth of material prosperity; that whistle sounds in a very different world today.

The old railway began its life in 1865, to enable slate from the mountains to be brought down to an outlet on the coast. Shunning the then inadequate road and taking a remarkably straight course up the valley of the Afon Fathew, the railway occupied a ledge on the lower slopes of the green

mountains as it climbed a gentle gradient towards its passenger terminus at Abergynolwyn. A short distance on at Nant Gwernol (where a new passenger terminus has now been built), funiculars rose to the drab quarries of Bryn Eglwys. This seemingly timeless existence continued until the quarries shut in 1946. A historic situation was about to arise; the Talyllyn was soon to become the world's first preserved steam railway.

The crunch point came in 1950 when the railway's owner, Sir Henry Haydn Jones, died. By this time the line was in a parlous state, its track kept in gauge by the turf growing between the rails, only one of its two engines, the

venerable *Dolgoch*, workable, several 1865 four-wheeled coaches well past their best, and no slate traffic; the main income was from summer tourists once more flooding to the seaside after years of wartime austerity. In those last days before Sir Haydn's death, the railway had a ghost-like atmosphere, its antique form winding among the trees and undergrowth hemming in the grass-grown track. Three days a week the traveller had ample time to see the magnificent scenery as the speed of the train rarely exceeded 8 or 9 mph – it was too risky to go faster. Flies, bees, butterflies and other insects wandered in and out of the open windows of the coaches and from time to time long

A scene on the 2 ft 3 in gauge Talyllyn Railway in 1953, two years after its takeover by the Talyllyn Railway Preservation Society. The engine at the then eastern terminus at Abergynolwyn, just 7 miles up the valley of the Afon Fathew from its coastal terminus at Tywyn, is 0-4-2 No. 3, recently acquired from the Western Region of British Railways and one-time mainstay of the Corris Railway further down the coast. No. 3 was named *Sir Haydn* after the long-time owner of the Talyllyn Railway.

147

1863-built 0-4-0 saddle tank *Prince* heads a Festiniog Railway special to celebrate publication of a book about the 150th anniversary; it makes a spirited run-past for the invited guests at Lyn Ystradau on 26 April 1987. *Prince* and *Princess*, built by George England and Co., were the first steam locomotives to be used successfully on so slim a gauge and were the progenitors of all narrow-gauge steam power the world over.

to tread among the Welsh. At that time no such organization had ever assumed the responsibility for running a railway and there was no shortage of prophets of doom who doubted the ability of volunteers to face the mountainous arrears of maintenance, to raise the vast sums of money that would be needed or to persevere through the inevitable setbacks with no motive other than sentiment and idealism. And there was a melancholy precedent from America, where the Bridgton & Harrison, a 2 ft gauge line in Maine, had been taken over by just such a band of enthusiasts and had collapsed in a matter of months in 1941 – although it remains the father of literally hundreds of preserved railways the world over.

While the Talyllyn was beginning to flourish again under new management, the famous Festiniog lay derelict,

brambles scraped along their sides. The railway was still regularly used by people from the few farms near the line, far from a bus route, who chattered together in Welsh unconcerned at the curious stares of any foreign (English) tourists.

The Talyllyn Railway was rescued from its coffin in a novel way. With the closure of the more famous Festiniog Railway to the north in 1946, it had become the oldest steam-hauled passenger-carrying narrow-gauge railway in the world and one man was determined that it would not be allowed to die. Author and canal preservationist, L. T. C. Rolt, along with two colleagues called a now historic meeting in Birmingham in October 1950, in which he set out his hopes for a possible future; from this the Talyllyn Railway Preservation Society was formed, the author becoming its first secretary. Looking back, it was a classic example of fools rushing in; angels would certainly have feared having shut its doors in 1946 when a last ship had called in at Porthmadog and taken on a load of slates. On 1 August that year the men were given notice as they put one of the original engines, the ageing *Princess*, into the shed, and the railway became a dismal and depressing sight. But the flame lit by Rolt made people wonder if the miracle could be repeated and in the autumn of 1951 the Festiniog Railway Society was founded. The problem was a far more formidable one than it had been at Tywyn. While the Talyllyn Railway Company had been wholly owned by Sir Haydn Jones, who had been sympathetic to the aims of the preservation society and whose executors therefore made a gift of control of it, the Festiniog was a statutory company whose shares were held by different owners and which moreover

Festiniog Railway's 2-6-2 Alco-built *Mountaineer* climbs out of Tan-y-bwlch on 24 August 1985. Rebuilt by the team at Boston Lodge Works, this machine has been transformed from a locomotive giving an erratic performance into one that is 100 per cent reliable, with power output increased by 40 per cent.

The Festiniog Railway was Great Britain's premier narrow-gauge line until its closure in 1946. It was reopened in part by preservationists in 1955 and subsequently in sections until the whole line from Porthmadog to Blaenau Festiniog was open to traffic (including a newly built deviation section to avoid an electricity power station lake). Today the FR is Great Britain's finest tourist-attuned narrow-gauge line. It is the proud possessor of 0-4-0 + 0-4-0 Fairlie double-articulated engines, one of which, *Merddin Emrys*, is seen here in 1961 with a Tan-y-Bwlch-bound train prior to the extension beyond that mountain village and the construction of the deviation. *Merddin Emrys* was rebuilt in the FR's Boston Lodge works.

Above: Aberystwyth station with a 2 ft 0 in gauge Vale of Rheidol train standing in the old Carmarthen platform. The engine is No.8 *Owain Glyndwr*, one of the two 2-6-2 tanks built specially for this section by the Great Western Railway and based on the original Davies and Metcalfe design. The Rheidol line is the only steam section of British Rail; it is currently on the market seeking a private purchase.

was heavily in debt. In short, the railway had a value as scrap metal far higher than it had as a going concern. But just as the Talyllyn could not be disposed of without an Act of Parliament to close it, neither could the Festiniog, and the whole matter became deadlocked until the money to pay off the creditors could be found. The saviours came in the form of Alan Pegler and a team of enthusiasts who later became the directors of the railway: they raised the money and negotiated – with considerable skill – with the interested parties, and the new Festiniog Railway was born, to become a flourishing concern whose story has been not only a saga of success but also the subject of a fascinating book in itself.

The difference in the founding of the Festiniog parallels its geography; the mountains through which it runs are those of Snowdonia, rugged and less friendly than those in the south. Altogether this is much more of a real railway; trains are vacuum-braked throughout, they include buffet cars in their consists and there is a workshop capable of not only rebuilding but also building locomotives. It is an old railway with a modern idiom, selling

computerized tickets on the one hand but when possible keeping, within the limits of a commercial concern, a solid link with history on the other.

The success of the Talyllyn and Festiniog Railways led to other imitators, as well as to the retention – albeit somewhat grudgingly – of British Rail's only narrow-gauge and sole steam-operated line, the Vale of Rheidol out of Aberystwyth, climbing up to Devil's Bridge, 207 m (680 ft) above sea level. In 1967 the author and some colleagues were asked by the then General Manager of British Rail's London Midland Region if they could find someone to take this lovely railway off his hands, rather on the basis of King Henry II exclaiming to his knights of Thomas à Becket 'Who will rid me of this base turbulent priest?'. It was not to be, as politics dictated differently, although today the wheel may well be turning full circle once more as the portents indicate a further desire to sell by British Rail. Time alone will tell.

All the Welsh lines have a marketing strategy under the name of Great Little Trains of Wales. The most dramatic of them is the Snowdon Mountain (which is now toying with diesels) and the

Right: The preserved ex-London-Brighton and South Coast section of railway deep in rural Sussex was one of the country's first standard-gauge tourist railways and it generally keeps its rural branch-line character. The railway has extensive workshops at Sheffield Park, where many one-time Southern Railway engines have been rebuilt. To show these off special Cavalcade Days are organized from time to time; on 27 June 1982 Schools Class 4-4-0 No. 928 *Stowe* and U class Mogul No. 1618 head the 11.27 train to Horsted Keynes through Three Arches cutting.

Opposite top: Bristol Temple Meads station on 17 October 1965: the train is a Stephenson Locomotive Society special which has worked down from Birmingham using 0-6-0 pannier tank No. 6435 and 7029 *Clun Castle*. It is the last year of steam on the Western Region of British Railways and *Clun Castle*'s fate still remains in the balance; final purchase was not until January 1966. No. 6435 has already been saved and is on her way down to the Dart Valley Railway at Totnes, a convenient, happy and cheap way of working the engine to its new home.

Right: Early days on the Dart Valley Railway in south Devon when the leased section from Buckfastleigh to Ashburton (now part of the A38 dual carriageway) was still open: ex-GWR 0-6-0 pannier tank No. 6435 crosses Salmon Leap bridge, Buckfastleigh, while taking two auto trailers to Ashburton on 14 July 1969.

gentlest the Welshpool and Llanfair in Montgomeryshire, once appropriately known as the 'Farmer's Line'. Had it not been for the enterprise of the few who took that step into the unknown in October 1950, these and other lines elsewhere could well have gone to the scrapman's torch.

While all the tourist lines in Wales are narrow gauge, those operating in England and Scotland are sections of what were once part of the nationalized system, branch lines closed under the Beeching or other forms of railway axe-wielding. There is one exception, the charming 3 ft 0 in gauge Isle of Man Railway, which operates one leg of a once three-legged system on the island between Douglas and Port Erin.

This is not the place to list the preserved railways of the world but mention must be made of those which have made their mark on history, including the first standard-gauge line to open as such in England, the

Below: Once an inhabitant of Barry scrapyard, ex-GWR 2-6-2 tank No. 4588 takes a train from Paignton to Kingswear over the southern section of the Dart Valley Railway. Though this and the Totnes to Buckfastleigh sections are under the same ownership, they operate as two quite separate systems. Kingswear was once the terminus of the Torbay express from Paddington, trains running through behind large 4-6-0s. Today the largest engine in traffic is a small-wheeled Manor but the atmosphere is still Great Western.

Bluebell Railway in Sussex. This section of BR's track was an early victim of what has been popularly known as the 'Beeching Axe'. It reopened after abortive attempts to keep the old line running; determined opponents to closure had even discovered that its original Act of Parliament required certain stations to be kept open in perpetuity so British Rail had had to go to the expense of asking Parliament's permission to close – it was given. The Bluebell Railway has two great advantages: it is within easy reach of London and it keeps up a strong Victorian atmosphere, which appeals both to the enthusiast and the general public. It has wisely concentrated on its old connection with the one-time Southern Railway and it runs through the gentle Sussex countryside.

With the happy launch of the Bluebell line, other work behind the scenes led to an announcement in the *Western Morning News* of 26 June 1964 that a new company, the Dart Valley Light Railway Limited, was about to be formed. Its objective was to 'acquire all or any interest in the railway now

Right: One-time GWR 2-6-2 tank No. 4555 leaves Buckfastleigh for Staverton and Totnes (Riverside) in the early days of the Dart Valley Railway. The two period-piece clerestory-roofed coaches had not yet been restored but the engine had received an overhaul at Swindon works.

existing between Totnes and Ashburton'. This somewhat bold statement led to the formation of the first private limited company to acquire and run a section of British Railways for pleasure purposes on a commercial basis. The Dart Valley, besides its line from Totnes to Buckfastleigh (originally it went as far as Ashburton), is now the possessor of another Devon branch, that from the popular seaside resort of Paignton to Kingswear opposite Dartmouth. Success has ensured that it is now a public company. Trains are painted in the old colours of the Great Western Railway, dark green for the engines and chocolate and cream for the coaches. The old company slogan 'Go Great Western' certainly applies to the Dart Valley.

Above: Arley station on the Severn Valley Railway in Worcestershire, one of Great Britain's premier tourist railways and an ex-Great Western Railway cross-country branch line. Rescued by preservationists, the Severn Valley is as near as possible a recreation of the past: stations, signals, stock and locomotives all represent everything that was good on an English country railway.

Others have followed suit and particular mention should be made of another ex-Great Western branch, this time in the West Midlands, now the Severn Valley Railway running from a junction with British Rail at Kidderminster to the old Shropshire town of Bridgnorth via Bewdley and the valley of the River Severn. Owned by literally thousands of small shareholders and with a very large volunteer element, the Severn Valley is a shining example of what can be done with sheer determination. To ride a train

from the brand new period-piece station at Kidderminster over the line to Bridgnorth is the nearest one can get to rail travel of the 1930s. And it has all been done for love.

Great Britain has so many steam tourist lines that special books are prepared to give them complete coverage. They include the Keighley and Worth Valley, where they made the film of The Railway Children, the Mid-Hants in luscious southern England, the North Yorkshire Moors, the North Norfolk, the Strathspey in Scotland, two 15 in gauge lines – the Ravenglass and Eskdale, and the Romney Hythe and Dymchurch. So it goes on.

Left: The attractive setting of Berwyn station on 7 September 1986, with the arrival of ex-GWR 0-4-2 tank No. 1466 (on loan from the Great Western Society's depot at Didcot) at the head of the 15.00 train from Llangollen. This was once a GWR cross-country line linking Ruabon with the Cambrian Railways' system at Dolgellau. It closed in 1966, leaving the track bed and stations to nature's mercy. This railway is a fine piece of restoration, sadly isolated from any main-line connection.

Opposite top: Ex-LNWR 0-6-2 coal tank No. 1054 leaves Bewdley with the 10.00 Bridgnorth to Kidderminster train on 20 September 1986. The locomotive has been repainted in its original LNWR colours, while the coaching stock is in LMS red. This is very much a country railway scene with the signalman leaning out of his window holding the electric tablet for the next single line section.

Opposite bottom: A scene at Didcot Railway Centre, Berkshire, during the Great Western Society's 25th anniversary celebrations on 1 June 1985. This unusual sight of standard- and broad-gauge trains passing one another is due to the loan of the replica 7 ft 0 in gauge *Iron Duke* made for the Science Museum, London, partly from pieces of an old 'Austerity' 0-6-0 saddle tank. The *Iron Duke* is just leaving on its mixed-gauge line while a Great Western small-wheeled 2-6-2 tank No. 5572 is busying itself on the local train service at Didcot Halt.

157

A comparatively early scene (though little changed today) of the North Yorkshire Moors Railway at Grosmont. To the left is the Eastern Region line from Middlesborough to Whitby. This long, one-time North Eastern Railway cross-country branch is a scenic operation based largely on LNER practice, though running trains with a variety of locomotive stock, including an ex-GWR 56XX class 0-6-2 tank. The locomotive heading the train is an ex-Lambton, Hetton and Joycey Colliery Railway 0-6-2 tank, while that on the right is almost a local – ex-NER Q6 class 0-8-0 No. 3395.

The bay platform used by Keighley and Worth Valley trains with two ex-LMS Stanier class 5 4-6-0s double-heading a train up the steeply graded tourist line to Haworth and Oxenhope. No.5025 on the left is in LMS livery, while the pilot engine No. 45212 is in British Railways' colours and numbering. This evocative scene might well date to around 1949 but it was in fact photographed in the mid-1970s.

IRELAND

The story of main-line steam preservation in Ireland is told later in the book but one pipe-dream come true has been the result of determination by enthusiasts in the far south of Eire in Tralee. Back in the early 1950s the Tralee and Dingle section of the CIE (Irish State Railways), a 3 ft gauge light railway built in 1891, was one of the last pieces of adventurous railroading left in Ireland. Constructed to a minimal budget and linking Tralee with the villages of West Kerry *en route* to the little port of Dingle, it crossed the Sleive Mish mountains, holding on to life by a fragile thread – the poor roads in the area and the need to move cattle from the Dingle peninsular once a month on the occasion of Dingle Fair. By then there were three engines only, all Hunslet-built 2-6-0 tanks supplied to the original Tralee and Dingle Railway. They needed the abilities of Kerry goats to do their job. In fact the Tralee and Dingle engines were sturdy, popular machines, which led to surplus locomotives being exported to other 3 ft gauge sections of CIE where further motive power was needed; one of them – moved to the Cavan and Leitrim section based at Ballinamore in County Leitrim close to the border with the Six Counties – was the sole 2-6-2 tank No. 5T. When that line closed in 1951 two American enthusiasts, the late Rogers Whitaker and Edgar Mead, purchased No. 5T along with a C&L 4-4-0 tank and had them shipped to Boston, with the 2-6-2 tank going to Steamtown, Bellows Falls, Vermont, as a static exhibit where it stayed rather unloved until plans were made to move the whole exhibition to Scranton, Pennsylvania, in 1985. By now that great writer and enthusiast Rogers Whitaker had died and Edgar Mead anxiously began looking for a new home for No. 5T.

This news reached a Tralee-based group of enthusiasts, the Great Southern Railway Preservation Society, and through one of its members' love of narrow gauge and the Tralee and Dingle Railway in particular the

idea of bringing the 2-6-2 tank home was born. Eventually, after a lot of transatlantic telephone calls, telexes and letters, the plan began to take shape and thanks to the Atlantic Container Line and some tolerant trucking and craneage people the engine made its way home. It now resides in Tralee, though plans are in hand for its movement to Mallow where the Great Southern Railway Preservation Society will begin restoration to working order. There can be no question of putting back the 30 miles plus of the old 3 ft gauge trackage but the formation is still intact from Tralee to Blennerville – a distance of only 2¼ miles. A former Isle of Man 3 ft gauge coach has been acquired and two original T&D vehicles in a restorable state have also been located. So maybe before long another 'impossible' restoration will have been made and the sound of a shrill whistle will echo back from the green mountains of Kerry; No. 5T will be on her way.

One-time Tralee and Dingle Railway Hunslet-built 2-6-2 tank No. 5 on temporary display in a timber yard at Tralee in 1987. Rescued from scrap by two American enthusiasts and taken to Steamtown, Vermont, No. 5 has now come back home. It is hoped that the engine will soon be at work over a short section of this west of Ireland 3 ft 0 in gauge railway.

Below: Headed by 0-6-6-0 Mallet tank No. 404, a weekend steam train follows the gorge of the river Doux in the high Massif between Tournon and Lamastre in July 1982. With its proximity to Lyons and its magnificent scenery, coupled with the small town of Lamastre's reputation as a gourmet centre, this highly successful railway has a solid future ahead.

FRANCE

In Europe they do things differently, each country to its own. The French were among the first to see the light and long before the notes of the last klaxon horn of the Vivarais railcars had echoed away into the Massif, the preservationists were active. When this metre-gauge Reseau closed in 1968, it was almost certain that one section between Tournon on the banks of the Rhone and Lamastre, a hill town of some gastronomic reputation, would reopen. And it did. That year more than 10,000 people rode up through the ravines of the Doux to Lamastre. Within five years trains were fully booked for the whole summer and some ferocious scrabbling around was necessary to locate, transport and refurbish additional coaching stock. The layman may well wonder just why the Vivarais should be so successful, for the tourists did not come in the old days. However, everything is now oriented to take tourists *up* from the Rhone Valley, giving them a day out and luring the Lyonnais towards something he really wants. What does he do in Lamastre? He EATS, for this is the gastronomic capital of the region

and to quote a well-known red book, 'vaut le voyage'. Thus, on a summer Sunday La Barratero, Le Commerce and Les Négociants burst at the seams and if one is on the relief train the penalty may well be a meal in one of the other restaurants or bars, although standards have risen to such a stage that it is almost impossible to get a substandard meal anywhere. When it is over the now replete narrow-gauge travellers rise, in time for the 4 p.m. Le Mastrou to take them down the valley with no worries about driving under the influence. The future of such a line seems assured when it can haul a

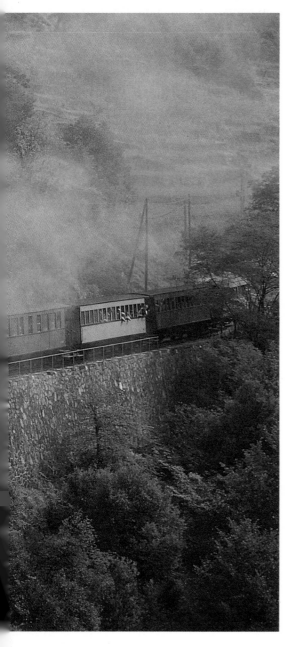

thousand hungry Gauls a weekend and return them home happy.

The fact that England, or rather Wales, was almost certainly the father of this pioneering spirit of preservation can become a trifle wearying to those who feel that, once sired, children should be left on their own. Even so the relationship continues, and in March 1970 the *Talyllyn News*, the magazine of the Talyllyn Railway Preservation Society, carried this letter from Monsieur J. Arrivetz:

As President of the Chemin de Fer Touristique de Meyzieu narrow gauge preservation society and working company, I must point out a fact which will, I am sure, interest the Talyllyn and Festiniog Railway Societies. In the summer of 1968, I went for journeys on the TR and FR. I was already President of the little Meyzieu line, near Lyons, a 1½-mile-long undertaking of 60 cm gauge, with seven steam locomotives and two diesels. I was most impressed with the Welsh narrow gauge and, back in France, I thought it might be possible to do better than before and gave my CFTM Council a detailed report about your wonderful concerns.

Three months later, the well-known Vivarais network, 50 miles south of Lyons, was closed by the Government because of a serious money shortage. Soon, we asked about preserving and reopening a part of it, from Tournon (Rhone Valley) to Lamastre (Ardeche). It was very difficult, and no one in authority thought it would be possible to work such a rural line purely as a tourist carrier. We argued for eight months, and one of our best arguments was to show photographs of crowds queuing for, and boarding the trains, at Tywyn and at Porthmadog, and these made the local authorities sit up and think. Eventually, we received authority to work the line from June 15th, 1969.

Then days after, our first steam train climbed along the line. In four months, without any advertising (it

Smart in a livery of deep-red, Swiss-built 0-6-6-0 Mallet tank No. 404 waits alongside the water column at Tournon on the Rhone Valley in July 1982. The metre-gauge Vivarais system, once over 160 km long and with three legs, is now a leading tourist operation using locomotives, stock and railcars belonging to its former owners but only over the short section from Tournon to Lamastre.

the success of the Talyllyn and Festiniog Railways, our project would have failed. Indirectly, your good work has preserved for posterity the most wonderful of the French light railways, and I am delighted to acknowledge it. To pay tribute of recognition and gratitude, you may advise your members that in 1970, every member of the Talyllyn or Festiniog Railway Societies, will, on showing his or her membership card, be granted children's fares on the Vivarais line, of seven francs instead of fifteen for a return trip in a steam train.

The trip on the Vivarais takes half a day. Trains leave Tournon on Saturdays and Sundays (and possibly on Thursdays) at 10.00 and 14.40 with extras as the traffic demands. We would be delighted to see you.

It was a most welcome tribute.

Once France was full of narrow-gauge railways but by the end of the 1960s most were gone. Those which remain are railcar-operated, though still adventurous, for the drivers tend to have the same habits as Frenchmen on the road. Nevertheless steam still survives: the Chemin de Fer de Provence out of Nice has an ex-Reseau Breton 4-6-0 tank and a Portuguese 2-4-6-0 Mallet tank; the CF de La Baie de Somme has once more come to life; and the Dunieres to St. Agreve section of the Vivarais is also preserved as a tourist line using an ex-P. O. Correze 0-4-4-0 Mallet tank. All ensure that the inner man is well catered for.

THE LOW COUNTRIES

The Low Countries too have their share of working steam lines, with Holland to the fore. There are basically three types of operation here, exemplified by the Hoorn-Medemblik (standard-gauge branch) Rotterdam steam tram (only about two km of this once huge 3 ft 6 in gauge tramway now exists) and very occasional main-line

was too late for this to be effective), we carried 12,000 passengers. We now run a winter service, with diesel railcars, and already 1970 looks like being 'passenger expansion year'. Our Chemin de Fer du Vivarais is 33 km (20 miles) long, through difficult country, in a landscape quite similar to the Welsh mountains. The line has four big viaducts, two tunnels, and six stations. The gauge is one metre. We have two Mallet steam locomotives, 0-6-0 + 0-6-0, and expect at least another three from other lines; two diesel locomotives; four railcars; seven passenger coaches (more on the way); and some 60 wagons.

I must acknowledge that, without

Left: The Belgian class 12 4-4-2 has a number of unusual features; it was the last class of inside cylinder engines ever to be built for express work, as well as the last Atlantic wheel arrangement. Built in 1939 to work fast three-coach trains over the Brussels to Ostend route, No. 12.004 was restored to working order in the early 1980s, hauling a series of special trains to commemorate 150 years of Belgian Railways. This photograph shows the engine crossing the river Meuse shortly after leaving Namur on 24 August 1985.

Below: Some 40 km north of Amsterdam the NS (Dutch State Railways) freight-only branch from Hoorn to Medemblik is now host to an attractive steam operation using 0-4-0 tanks, including an attractive tram-type locomotive from the Limburg Tramway. This is seen here leaving Hoorn with a set of ex-Austrian coaches in July 1975.

steam where the ultimate glory is a truly beautiful Beyer Peacock 4-6-0 which normally resides in the Railway Museum at Utrecht. Belgium sports a few State Railway preserved engines, including a streamlined Atlantic and a Pacific, while in the Flemish part of the country the Stoomspoorlijn Dendermonde-Puurs (using a vertical boilered 0-4-0) makes occasional journeys, a reminder of the many minor lines which once criss-crossed the country. Last but not least comes Luxembourg, where the Grand Duchy's sole preserved railway is tucked away in the south-west corner of the country at Rodange. This standard-gauge line uses a couple of tank engines with some SNCB and CFL stock.

Above: The Grand Duchy's sole preserved railway lies in the south-western corner of the country at Rodange, near the meeting with the frontiers of France and Belgium, and is standard gauge. Operation is on Sundays and most national holidays. Here 0-6-0 tank No. 9 *Anna* (Hohenzollern 2227/08) leaves Fond de Gras station with a train for Rodange on 7 September 1986.

Right: Once steam had departed from regular use on West German tracks, authority deemed it gone for good but relented to cover the 150th anniversary celebrations in 1985. These were based on Nurnberg, with special trains running to a regular timetable, an extremely efficient piece of organization. Restored 2-6-2 No. 23.105 heads the 10.20 excursion from Nurnberg to Amberg on 28 July 1985.

WEST GERMANY AND AUSTRIA

West Germany and Austria have recently come to life with steam on their respective State Railway tracks, the Germans making the experiment while celebrating their 150th anniversary in 1985 after some years of a complete ban reminiscent of those dark days in Great Britain from 1968 to 1971. The Austrians, who have still kept very small pockets of live steam on their State Railway, the OBB, responded equally magnificently in their 150th year, 1987. Both countries have tourist steam lines, the majority in Austria being narrow gauge and those in Germany mostly standard.

Germany has one spectacular piece of tourist line which is only available through the courtesy of NATO. The Wutachtal Bahn lies in scenic south-west Germany and was originally built as long ago as 1890. It links the villages of Weizen and Blumberg, some ten kilometres apart, though this railway takes 26.5 kilometres to do the job with the help of one spiral, four hairpins, six tunnels and four major viaducts: the 1.7 km-long Stockhalde-Kreiskeh tunnel is the only railway spiral tunnel in Germany. The Wutachtal Bahn was never a busy line except during the two World Wars and with its obviously high mainten-ance costs it did not rate highly on the German State Railway's survival lists. Passenger services were withdrawn in

When the West German State Railways (DB) celebrated their 150th anniversary with a series of special trains, one of the more unusual of these was a demonstration freight – running from Nurnberg in the direction of Amberg using a class 50 2-10-0 No. 50.622. This was on 19 January 1986; earlier that day the same locomotive had been used on a passenger special.

Two evocative shots of Krauss 0-6-2 tank No. 3 running on 30 December 1983. *Right*: The 10.30 Jenbach-Mayrhofen soon after leaving Jenbach. *Opposite*: The same train in silhouette under the snow-covered mountain slopes towards Zell am Ziller.

1955 after damage to a tunnel but for an unknown reason (at least to this author) NATO decided that the line had some strategic importance – its original purpose was to avoid a railway incursion into Switzerland – and in 1962 ordered the repair of the tunnel and a total renewal of the signalling. The works were completed by 1963 but the line never reopened for normal traffic, though it has been leased by the State Railway to the Museumbahn Wutachtal which operates its trains.

With such a spectacular route climbing through the wooded hills, its tourist appeal is high and trains run each summer. 1987 saw some steam spectaculars over the Easter period, including the running of ex-Prussian P38 class 4-6-0 No. P8 1772, though this unfortunately met with an accident, derailing itself on some points. The

year 1990 however is the Wutachtal's centenary and a visit must be high on any enthusiast's calendar.

One of the places which is a 'must' on any visit to Austria is Jenbach, a short distance east of Innsbruck, where they build diesel and electric locomotives in the Jenbacher Werke. Jenbach is a country railway centre and one of considerable note for not only does one see the occasional Kreigslok 2-10-0 (complete with Giesl ejector) trundling through on the standard-gauge line but there are also two tourist narrow-gauge railways. The older of the two lines is the metre-gauge Achenseebahn, not the least remarkable thing about which is that it is owned by the Tyrolean Water Works Company. Built in 1888, it is only 7.2 kilometres long and during recent years it has only run in summer; but its

One of West Germany's most scenic tourist operations runs over the Wutachtal Bahn between Weizen and Blumberg in the south-west of the country. On 17 April 1984, celebrating ten years of its preservation, a special train was hired by a television company and headed by P8 class No. 38.1772, one of the historic ex-Prussian Railway designed 4-6-0s; it is shown here crossing Wutach Brucke viaduct with a Blumberg-bound train. Sadly the locomotive split the points a few minutes later when approaching Epfenhoffen station; the track damage was repaired within hours but the engine needed expensive repair.

trains are still the originals. The railway owns three rack and adhesion 0-4-0Ts (two of 1888 and one built 15 years later), which still haul the original four-wheeled wooden coaches – in fact they are almost living dinosaurs, like the Shay in the Philippines.

A second remarkable thing about this line is that it uses the rather unusual Riggenbach rack system in which a close-runged metal ladder between the rails replaced the twin opposed-tooth rack rails of the more common Abt system; this ladder is engaged by toothed wheels under the locomotive which are connected by a complicated system of gearing and connecting rods to four ordinary adhesion driving wheels. The cylinders drive the whole assembly through a wheel about 30 cm (1 ft) off the ground, which is so arranged that when the engine is in motion it revolves rapidly in the wrong direction. Not only is this an interesting optical demonstration, it is also an equally fascinating audible one as the gearing makes grinding-whining noises reminiscent of an elderly tramcar.

The train starts conventionally enough (considering its peculiarity) from a bay platform at Jenbach OBB station and immediately after reaching the outer limits of the yard it hits the rack section and begins to climb; fairly easily at first, a mere 1 in 10 across open

Eisenbahn-Kurier (EK) No. 38 1772, a classic 4-6-0 built by Schichau in 1915, comes off its train at Konigstein after arriving from Frankfurt on 10 November 1985.

169

An Achenseebahn train beginning the ascent out of Jenbach with a train for Eben in the early 1970s. Because this first section is rack-worked, the 0-4-0 tank pushes its train up the hill into the woods. The rack is clearly visible between the rails beyond the guard's open door.

Above: Austria was a couple of years behind Germany with her railway building and consequently the 150th anniversary celebrations there did not take place until 1987. Unfortunately these were not graced by good weather but the excellent events included runs behind some extremely geriatric locomotives, as exemplified here. Graz-Koflacher Bahn 0-6-0 No. 671, shown near Rosental, takes a charter special from Graz Hbf to Koflach on 3 September 1987.

fields, but later at 1 in 6 or 1 in 5 through the forest. Two four-wheeled coaches are a full load and they make the engine bellow very fiercely as it forges up the gradient at a steady walking pace under a tall column of black smoke. In just over three kilometres and 28 minutes the train, having climbed 550 m (1,800 ft), suddenly moves on to the level and at a tiny loop the engine – which has been pushing so far – runs round its coaches and prepares to pull them. The second part of the journey is gently downhill through Maurach village to a pier on the mountain lake at Eben.

Perhaps another oddity about the Achenseebahn is that it is still there, even if only running in summer, for the Austrian government some 20 or so years back and at enormous expense built a road up from Jenbach to Pertisau on the opposite side of the lake from Eben which can make the trip in half the time. However, the crowds of summer tourists are sensible enough to leave the Achenseestrasse alone as an alien and unwarranted

Far left: Two German-built class 52 2-10-0s No.s 52.7594 and 52.855, standard Austrian freight power for over 40 years (though also used on some branch-line and local passenger workings), head Tour D-Vienna-Wiener Neustadt-Puchberg near Unter Hoflein on the outward run on 5 September 1987. The train engine is fitted with a Giesl exhaust ejector and flat chimney, a device reducing back pressure and giving a multiple orifice exhaust, allowing the use of poor-quality fuel. In later years a large number of OBB locomotives were so fitted.

intrusion, and use the train and lake steamer for their half-day excursion. So with luck the dinosaurs will be making their thunderous way up to Eben for years yet, disregarding the fact with dignity that their driving wheels appear to be going round the wrong way.

Across the tracks and the main road from the State Railway's station are the sheds and offices of quite a different railway, the 760 mm gauge Zillertal-bahn dating from 1901 and running on the floor of an Alpine valley to Mayrhofen, which is a ski centre in winter. Translated, the Zillertalbahn means Silver Valley Railway, a nice enough name for any line. The Zillertal is not just a tourist line; it has a solid year-round business running freight and passenger trains by diesel traction, though it was 100 per cent steam until the late 1960s. Today, because tourism pays off, some of the nice little Krauss 0-6-2 tanks have been maintained and run on scheduled services both in high summer for the tourists and mid-winter for the skiers. A ride on this railway, although spectacular, is less scenically dramatic than on the Achenseebahn because the mountains keep their distance, although the last few kilometres are at a steady 1 in 40 so the steam locomotives have to work hard to keep up with the brisk timetable.

Austria is still full of such lines, most

working only in summer. These include two steam-operated mountain rack lines of a more conventional nature than the Achenseebahn and a number of narrow-gauge railways kept in circulation for one reason only – the number of tourists who want the experience of a ride over them.

SWITZERLAND

Of all countries in Europe, Switzerland took tourism to its heart early, but this is a land of clean swish electrics where steam was banished long ago. Even so there has been serious rethinking to catch modern nostalgia both on the minor and not so minor railways as well as on some rack lines. Of these a stalwart supporter of steam traction is the Brienzer Rothorn (Red Peak) Cog Railway.

The Brienz line was the first purely mountain railway in the Bernese Oberland, opening in 1892 and running 7.6 kilometres from Brienz on the shore of the lake with the same name to the mountain top, a climb of over 1,500 m (5,000 ft) capped by breathtaking views as the train climbs. The engines are from the Swiss Locomotive Works (where else?) and work on the Abt system. Other mountain lines which also use steam on an occasional but regular basis are the Rigi and Monte Generoso Railways.

Below: In the beginning steam reigned almost supreme on Switzerland's rack-worked mountain railways, though in most cases this was quickly superseded by electrification. Two notable exceptions were the Monte Generoso line near Lugano and the Brienz-Rothorn on Lake Brienz. The Monte Generoso (except for the odd special) has now turned itself over to more modern power but the Rothorn rack still reverberates to the sound of steam, albeit with a diesel or two lurking for the unwary. Trains are shown here passing at Planalp in the early 1970s, when the railway was still 100 per cent steam.

One of the larger non-state railways in Switzerland to retain a modicum of steam for special excursions is the Rhaetian Railway or Rhatishe Bahn, linking such famous resorts as St. Moritz and Davos. When these trains run they are truly spectacular occasions, using a couple of the line's preserved 2-8-0s which twist and climb their way through the valleys. This photograph shows one such train behind Nos. 107 and 108 on the Rhaetian main line between Bergen and Alba.

But the star of them all is undoubtedly the Rhaetian Railway, an extensive metre-gauge network set in the mountainous south-east corner of Switzerland, linking such famous resorts as St. Moritz and Davos. There is no regular schedule for steam excursions on the Rhatishe Bahn, to give the railway its proper name, but these are chartered from time to time by groups of enthusiasts, usually on one- or two-day spectaculars for the system is over 270 kilometres in length. The journey can include four spiral tunnels and bridges of great beauty and boldness; the Landwasser Viaduct near Filisur, for example, is built on a sweeping curve and is over 60 m (200 ft) high, one arch being sprung beneath a tunnel mouth from a sheer precipice. The engines are 2-8-0s sometimes supplemented by a 2-6-0 tank.

SCANDINAVIA

Scandinavia has no coal but even so steam died comparatively hard here, lasting into the 1960s with various 'strategic reserves' kept for much longer – the final collection in Finland not being dispersed until 1987. Both the Norwegians and the Swedes were well in front with narrow-gauge tourist lines – the Sorumsand line in Norway and the Grafsnas-Anten plus the Jadnas Tallas in Sweden. Finland has the Humppila-Forssa, a section of the last independent narrow-gauge railway in the country, but more recently has run a regular series of main-line steam specials using Pacifics 2-8-2s and 2-8-0s, though their publicity has sadly been somewhat poor. These have been solidly historic trains with wood-panelled coaches.

NORTH AMERICA

Looking at the steam picture of North American tourism today it is hard to realize the bleak days of the late 1960s when so much seemed lost to the whole railroad scene. Like Tom Rolt who pioneered British railway preservation, there are those in the States who must be equally remembered today among the plethora of new schemes and the euphoria of main-line working giants. Perhaps the greatest pioneer was Ellis D. Attwood, a cranberry farmer in South Carver, Massachusetts. Like many fans now, Ellis was a narrow-gauge enthusiast, and like a number of others he deplored the gradual but permanent decline of those magnificent pieces of American folklore. But unlike most, he did something about it. As has been mentioned earlier, one of the first (but sadly abortive) efforts in railway preservation was to save the Bridgton & Harrison 2 ft gauge line in Maine in 1941. Ellis saw the débâcle but managed to purchase some 2-4-4 tank locomotives plus a few pieces of rolling stock and put them into store. When the Second World War ended he hit on the idea of building a railway on his estate along the dykes of the cranberry bogs to provide useful transportation within the farm. But with the tracks laid and the engines steaming, he had to think again; public demand as well as heavier than expected costs saw to that. Thus the idea of steam railways for pleasure was born. The memorable date is 7 April 1947, the day the last spike was ceremoniously driven and the Edaville Railway founded.

Ellis died tragically in an accident in 1950 but fortunately a distant relative of some wealth, F. Nelson Blount, whose money also came from a New England table delicacy – clams, bought Edaville and developed it. Sadly, he too died tragically when his private plane crashed in 1967. A new owner, George E. Bartholomew, took over in 1970 and progress is such that the little engines and their trains are likely to continue to give pleasure to many, as both his predecessors had wished.

Another of Blount's philanthropic schemes was the Steamtown Museum at Bellows' Falls, Vermont. Blount collected Canadian and American steam locomotives as others collect stamps or coins and before he died he had the wonderful idea of setting up a live steam centre with an operating railway connection. This he did using part of the old Rutland system, which

The late Ellis D. Attwood set up the 2 ft 0 in gauge Edaville Railroad on his cranberry farm as early as 1947 and although sadly Mr Attwood is no longer with us, his railway most certainly is. Very much a pioneer organization, the Edaville has collected motive power from long-gone narrow-gauge railroads in the United States, the Monson and the Bridgton & Harrison. This photograph shows locomotives from both lines double-heading a train in June 1980. Leading is 0-4-4 No. 3 from the Monson (Vulcan 1913); the train engine is Bridgton & Harrison 2-4-4 No. 7 (Baldwin 1913).

Above: One-time London and South Western Railway M7 class 0-4-4 tank carrying its British Railways' number 30053 stands on one of the roundhouse radiating roads at Steamtown, Bellows Falls, in June 1969. This engine has now been repatriated and can be found on the Swanage Railway (ex-Southern Railway) in Dorset undergoing restoration for return to service.

was taken over by Vermont State to prevent closure, operating the section from Bellows Falls to Rutland by arrangement. All this was fine while the clam millions lasted but after Blount's death, even though there was a financial foundation, Steamtown became a scene of some dereliction. Most locomotives and stock have now been removed to Scranton, Pennsylvania, and there is a little light in the darkness, plus a great deal of hope. The fiscal year of 1987 saw the sponsoring of a bi-partisan bill through the United States Congress and some $8 million has been appropriated to

protect the locomotives, which have been out in the open for 30 years or so. Plans are still tentative but this site at Scranton is that of the former Delaware, Lackawanna-Western Railroad's yard and works complex, most of which is intact. There are major plans in the pipeline and the Foundation's board expect the site to be designated one of national historic importance. Nelson Blount's dream is far from dead.

The steam scene in North America is encouraging and not only have such institutions as the Mount Washington Cog Railway survived unscathed but new enterprises have flourished throughout the land. A glance at the Bible of such operations, the *Steam Passenger Service Directory*, shows 191 short lines and active museums throughout the United States and Canada. There are main-line runs of such magnificent steeds as the Norfolk & Western class J 4-8-4, which was outshopped from Roanoke works as late as 1950 – the epitome of modern steam, and the huge class A 2-6-6-4 – No. 1218 of 1943, the world's second largest active steam locomotive, the prize going to the Union Pacific's *Challenger*. The Norfolk & Western 2-6-6-4 ran in revenue service until

1959 when it was sold out of service to Union Carbide, who used it as a stationary boiler.

By dint of providence (for he was an intensely religious man) the engine was rescued by Nelson Blount and sent to Steamtown. In 1968 it was leased back to the Norfolk & Western Railway, and moved to the Roanoke Transportation Museum. Recently, in 1985, Norfolk Southern (of which the N&W had been a part) made a gift of two diesels to the Foundation in exchange for an absolute title to No. 1218, and the engine was moved from the Museum to the new company's works at Birmingham, Alabama, for restoration which is reputed to have cost over $2 million. Its first run after restoration was on 21 April 1987. But sadly there is a *caveat*: insurance problems have recently hit American privately owned main-line steam and the position is not totally clear. During the summer of 1986 difficulties caused a number of cancellations but this may well have been only a hiccup, for 1987 saw few major problems. Let us hope that the scales are once more weighted evenly.

Opposite below: The Norfolk & Western Railway built the class J 4-8-4 from 1941, a modern, home-designed machine ready to compete with the diesel if given equal terms, capable of being fully serviced and turned round in an hour. Sadly one railway could not hold out alone and the Js went to the wall with the rest. But they were (and with the restoration to full working order of No. 611 still are) superb machines and an example of just what can be done. In her days of regular service No. 611 pulls out of Roanoke with the southbound 'Tenessean' on 6 November 1956.

Left: Said to be the largest, heaviest and most powerful engine ever to handle express passenger trains, this articulated 4-6-6-4 dates from 1936, with a further batch emerging between 1942 and 1944. Challengers headed Union Pacific trains between Salt Lake City, Las Vegas and Los Angeles at speeds well up to 70 mph and taking 20 coaches – a remarkable sight and even more memorable sound. Fortunately No. 9895 was kept as a static exhibit at Cheyenne, enabling it to be restored to full working order in 1981 and used on special excursions; it is seen here at Salt Lake City on 25 June 1982.

It is perhaps invidious to single out examples of tourist lines but two in Colorado are without doubt star performers: both were once part of a 3 ft gauge network worked by the Denver and Rio Grande Western and both are now privatized. During the 1950s many U.S. railroads were in a position of retrenchment, closing lines and cutting services, and the D&RGW was no exception: it sought an abandonment order over the spectacular Silverton branch out of Durango, Colorado, where the lure of silver had once dictated this expensive development. The company applied formally to the Interstate Commerce Commission (ICC) for the order and were refused on the grounds that 'the branch serves a distinct public need' and, significantly, that service on the line contributed 'a substantial profit to the applicants system'. This decision, made as late as 1962, put a cat among the pigeons, particularly as the company's policy had been that if its narrow-gauge lines were ignored, traffic would become discouraged and disappear.

From 1962 on, with no other choice open to it, the Denver and Rio Grande Western took it upon themselves to do something positive. They bought options on all property on both sides of Main Avenue, Durango, from the station up to Sixth Street, and planned an 'Old West' pioneer town attraction; it worked. New coaches were built at the company's Burnham shops, very much on the old pattern but all steel, and they set up shop. The ICC eventually allowed the line to be sold to private enterprise and now the service has been expanded to make it an all-year-round operation. To quote the *Steam Passenger Service Directory*, 'The train travels through the remote wilderness area of San Juan National Forest following the winding Animas River through breathtaking scenery accessible only by rail, on horseback or by foot. The 90-mile round trip to Silverton takes nine hours including a $2\frac{1}{4}$ hour stop for lunch. Advance reservation should be made to avoid disappointment.' What more can be said, except that the engines are authentic Alcos and Baldwin 2-8-2s

Opposite: For many years the Southern Railway was to the fore in running steam excursions, using medium-sized engines – 4-6-2, 2-8-4, 4-6-4, 2-10-4, etc. Following the merger with the Norfolk & Western to produce the Norfolk, Southern Corporation, two ex-N&W engines have been added to the steam roster. First came the J class 4-8-4 and then, in 1987, the A class 2-6-6-4. Primarily intended for fast freight work, the haulage of up to 25 coaches gives this fine locomotive no trouble at all. Here it accelerates away from a photo-stop near Dalton *en route* from Atlanta to Chattanooga on 7 November 1987.

Left: Mobile and Gulf RR 2-6-0 No. 97 (Baldwin 1925) at Browning, Alabama, in April 1966. This engine now works on the ten-mile-long French Lick, West Baden & Southern Railway running out of the old Monon RR station at French Lick, Indiana, the ride taking in pleasant wooded countryside and one of the United State's largest tunnels. This is the only steam locomotive on the line.

Durrango shed on the 3 ft 0 in gauge Denver and Rio Grande Western Railway one evening in September 1966 – in the days when access was available to all-comers. The engine standing to the left of the old wooden coaling stage is 2-8-2 No. 473 built by Alco in 1923 and still working today.

dating from 1923 to 1930, all formerly belonging to the Denver and Rio Grande Railroad. Even so, the new owners may well be having second thoughts; running a tourist railway is a relentless and expensive business.

The story does not end here, for the Silverton line was only a branch of a once extensive narrow-gauge network taking in the tracks from Alamosa, New Mexico, to Durango, Colorado. There was a 'main line' passing over the notorious Cumbres Pass at a height of 3,053 m (10,015 ft). Once Pullman and sleeper trains travelled this route but in 1951 the passenger service was suddenly dropped on the 'ignore it and it will go away' basis. But it did not go away as freight business boomed in the 1950s thanks to a huge oil exploration programme in the San Juan Basin. Long trains of oil pipes were moved

daily from Alamosa to Farmington in train loads of up to 70 cars, though by the mid-1960s this was down to perhaps two trips a week. A last chartered passenger train ran on Sunday, 9 October 1966 with 2-8-2 No. 484 and a string of yellow coaches, the railroad stating publicly that it would never run another. Final closure came in 1968.

Somewhat misled by the spectacular carryings on of the Silverton branch, the State governments of Colorado and New Mexico proceeded to purchase 64 of the most scenic miles of the D&RGW's Alamosa to Durango route – those from Antonito to Chama, including the Cumbres Pass, thus putting themselves in the *Guinness Book of Records* (or at least becoming eligible for it) by being in the somewhat unenviable position of having the

longest tourist railway in the world – 50 per cent longer than the already long Silverton line. The line is run by a concessionaire as the Cumbres and Toltec Scenic Railroad, with trains working daily from mid-June to mid-October. Because of the length some passengers make one journey only, returning by bus. The two daily trains meet at Osia, Colorado, for a somewhat al fresco lunch; the locomotives return to their home depots with the ongoing trains after turning on the wye. The ascent of the 1 in 25 Cumbres Pass taxes every ounce of tractive effort from the 1925-built Baldwin K36 class 2-8-2s (often doubleheaded at weekends) and the sound of the locomotive's exhaust coupled with

the chime whistling is a real delight to any steam enthusiast. Either way it can only be described as a fabulous ride. A winter bonus every other year includes a superb train spectacular when one of the old rotary snow ploughs is steamed up and propelled over part of the line by a pair of 2-8-2s: a supreme example of steam against the elements.

The Cumbres and Toltec Railroad is really a form of living museum and it is treated as such by the authorities who share the responsibility for its future. An interstate agency, the Cumbres and Toltec Scenic Railroad Commission, was created in 1977 to replace the complicated and somewhat cumbersome earlier custodians and operators, and this has outlined a five-year

Mikados 473 and 476 team up to take a heavy Durango to Silverton train along the mountain shelf approaching Rockwood in September 1983. This photograph illustrates vividly the sheer drop to the river valley and the reason for sending a motor-driven trolley ahead of the first train of the day in case of falling boulders. It is a long time since the old D&RGW had traffic necessitating doubleheading to Silverton.

Right: Baldwin 2-8-2 No. 487 climbs up from Chama with an Osia train on 27 August 1987. Like the Durango to Silverton line, this now privately owned 64-mile-long railway was once a vital communications link owned by the D&RGW. The magnificently scenic route ascends to 3,050 m (10,015 ft) at Cumbres summit, wild and desolate country in winter.

Opposite top: The Cumbres and Toltec Scenic Railroad has a quantity of ex-D&RGW wagons in its collection of stock (their original trains were made up from converted box cars) and some of these can be hired to make up a replica freight train for enthusiast photographic safaris. Such a train ran on 29 Augus 1987 and is seen here between Lobato and Cresco.

Opposite bottom: Denver and Rio Grande Western's K-36 class 2-8-2s Nos. 488 and 484 being oiled up at Chama, New Mexico, ready for a hard day's work over the famous 4 per cent grade towards the Cumbres Pass. Even today on the Toltec and Cumbres Railroad enthusiasts can wander the yards at Chama and Antonito to watch the ever fascinating scene of coaling, watering and generally making ready one of the world's most lifelike machines.

development plan to meet the demands of the future. Fortunately, passenger receipts have increased over recent years but these in turn provide problems of visitor accommodation, availability of locomotives and rolling stock, let alone the facilities at Osia where up to 500 people need to be fed at the midday halt. However, the museum railroad is investing in additional motive power as well as looking at solutions aimed at improving tourist arrangements. As the premier railroad magazine looking at steam preservation in the U.S.A., *Locomotive & Railway Preservation*, has pointed out, the Cumbres and Toltec trains are doing exactly what was expected of them 100 years ago.

For sheer professionalism one of the first preserved railways to operate, the Strasburg in Pennsylvania, takes some beating. This is a nine-mile, 45-minute round trip from Strasburg to, appropriately, Paradise through the lush farmlands of the Dutch country. The Railroad Museum of Pennsylvania is neatly adjacent to the Strasburg terminus. Another line which takes a lot of beating is the Cass Scenic Railway in West Virginia, using Shay-type geared locomotives over the 17-mile route from Cass to Bald Knob in the Allegheny Mountains. This is the old lumber railway running up the side of Cheat Mountain through spruce forests to the mountain top. It is an excellent example of local government today, with the Governor of West Virginia signing a bill to bring the old lumber line into the Cass State Parks system. Included in this deal were three Shay locomotives. Since the opening up to Bald Knob in 1968, this railway has gone from strength to strength and in 1978 the West Virginia Department of National Resources purchased the town of Cass itself, making a superb period-piece holiday complex. Over the years a worn-out logging complex that was about to be scrapped has been turned into a first-rate museum, not only keeping alive a priceless collection of antique geared locomotives but also providing an equally priceless educational public amenity.

A last look at U.S.A. tourist operations should be at one of its first – the Mount Washington Cog Railway which was formed in 1865; by 1867 the railway was ready for operation. This line was the brainchild of one Sylvester Marsh, a successful meat packer in Chicago who pioneered what was then called 'the railroad to the moon'. The first engine was a vertical boilered affair named *Hero*, but that was soon to be changed. To the non-enthusiast eye (and there were not many about in the mid-19th century), the vertical boilered engine looked rather like a large salt or pepper cruet and seeing it for the first time a visitor was heard to call it a 'peppersass'. The name stuck, though it was later refined to *Old Peppersass*. *Peppersass* was one of 16 locomotives built for the railroad, the most recent being completed as late as 1969 for the railway's centennial and named after

Small but excellent describes the five-mile-long Strasburg Railroad which runs most aptly to Paradise through the farmlands of Dutch Pennsylvania. This is one of the oldest and busiest steam tourist railways in the U.S.A., providing a half-hourly service at the height of the season. One of the line's earlier (and larger) locomotives is No. 90, a Baldwin 2-10-0 of 1924 which came from the English-sounding Great Western Railway.

187

Right: Three-truck Shay No. 7 (Lima 1921) at Cass, West Virginia, in June 1969. This is one of six Shays used on this scenic ex-logging railway now successfully turned to tourism; it also uses other geared locomotives – a Heisler and a Climax – thus showing off a bygone age. Passengers can ride the trains to Whittaker and Bald Knob up grades as steep as 11 per cent, including two switchbacks.

Opposite bottom: One of the United States' more authentic tourist railways is the 3 ft 0 in gauge East Broad Top Railroad running out of Rockhill Furnace close to Orbisonia, Pennsylvania. Saved from extinction by a benevolent scrap merchant, the railway does not run through particularly thrilling scenery but it is still the same today as it was prior to closure as a common carrier a quarter of a century ago. The East Broad Top was the last operating narrow-gauge line east of the Mississippi and ran for more than 80 years carrying freight, mail and passengers. All the locomotives are Baldwin 2-8-2s, including No. 12 (Baldwin 1911) seen here at Rockhill Furnace in January 1969.

the colourful Colonel Henry Teague who had bought the whole railway, lock, stock and barrel, in 1931 for $100,000. The ride itself is quite an adventure, for Mount Washington's weather record is variable and high winds are likely to carry off passengers' hats, handbags and even wigs. One unfortunate tourist dropped her handbag when she alighted from the train at the summit and stooping to pick it up, she found her light cotton dress snatched off over her head by the wind: luckily the dress snagged on a rock before it disappeared off the mountain top.

Above: The lower terminus of the Mount Washington Cog Railway in June 1969, showing a waiting train behind 0-2-2-0 cog locomotive aptly named *Base Station*; on static display is the world's first cog engine, *Old Peppersass*, looking rather like a steam wheelbarrow. The Mount Washington Cog Railway was the world's first mountain-climbing railway using a rack system.

More seriously, the Mount Washington Cog Railway is one of the world's most historic rack lines and the ride is more than just a trip up to the summit of a New Hampshire peak. It traverses what is still the steepest section of railway track in the world, the well-known Jacob's Ladder, a wooden trestle built into the mountainside with a grade of 37.4 per cent. The engines themselves are apparitions from another age and the railway has scarcely changed in the last 100 years, except of course for much more modern facilities for its tourist passengers. Like Snowdon Mountain Railway there is a restaurant at the top (if the weather allows the trains to make it) and like Snowdon the view may be good but the food is variable! Even though the Mount Washington Cog Railway is an antique, its safety record has been a good one, the rack and pinion principle being a universally accepted device. The cog wheels, as with other rack lines, also work on the train's descent using the compression in the engine's cylinders to hold the train back. Each engine has four sets of brakes and each coach two independent sets. The railway tells the story of a woman passenger who once asked a conductor, 'What happens if the brakes give out?' 'We've got

A scene in the wilderness of Mount Washington with two ascending trains passing a train on its way down to base. The bleak surroundings make clear the problems of winter maintenance and summer wind storms.

another set to put on, Ma'am.' 'Yes, but what happens if they all let go?' 'Well, Ma'am, that depends on the kind of life you've led.'

North in Canada operations are somewhat naturally more sparse, the star being the 40-mile run from Vancouver to Squamish. The round trip of 80 miles takes 5½ hours including an hour and a half at Squamish, a scenic journey along the coast with an island-dotted sea on the one side and mountains on the other. The locomotive is a glorious if rather

British Columbia Railway ex-Canadian Pacific 'Royal Hudson' 4-8-4 2860 on a tourist train running out of Vancouver to Squamish.

inappropriate one, a Canadian Pacific 'Royal Hudson' 4-6-4 No. 2860, one of the semi-streamlined variety which took his late Majesty King George VI and Queen Elizabeth across Canada in 1939. The class built by the Montreal Locomotive Works first came into service in 1937, some being fitted with locomotive boosters raising the tractive effort from 45,000 lb to 57,000 lb. One direct result of their introduction was the time saved by the reduction in locomotive changes needed to cross Canada from 14 to 9.

Other ex-Canadian steam includes the Prairie Dog Central at Winnipeg where No. 3, a Dubs & Co. Glasgow 4-4-0 of 1882, beautifully restored, works a 36-mile, two-hour round trip to Grosse Isle over the Oakpoint Subdivision of Canadian National Railways using vintage wooden coaches, and the ten-mile Salem and Hillsborough Railroad which offers its passengers trips on 'wine and dine' trains with excellent quality food – an example that some of its progenitors might usefully follow.

Baldwin-built (37083/11) 4-6-0 waits outside the overall roof at Sao Joao del Rei with a load of empty stone wagons in October 1977. This 2 ft 6 in railway was then in full working order, with its fleet of Baldwin 4-4-0, 4-6-0 and 2-8-0 locomotives kept in immaculate condition. Today the line is no longer a common carrier but it provides a superb example of Brazil's dedication to railway preservation.

SOUTH AMERICA

Somehow one does not expect to see tourist railways in South America but they do exist, the Machu Picchu line out of Cuzco being a prime example except that today steam is long gone. Chile has made some experiments in running main-line excursions out of Temuco and on the Longquimay branch in recent times, but it is Brazil which is in the lead with some very impressive preservation schemes, two of them of outstanding interest.

Sao Paulo, apart from having the doubtful distinction of being one of the most polluted cities in the world, is also host to a remarkable museum operation at Paranapiacaba, the restoration to working order of a section of a steam-operated cable railway, the famous 1 in 12 Santos or Serro de Mar incline. This is the first of two sections built to move merchandise from the

coffee-growing Sao Paulo plateau to the port of Santos in 1887, with a second parallel incline built in 1901. Because of heavy traffic the first section has been totally reconstructed, and now operates on the Abt system and is fully electrified; consequently it is now capable of taking everything on offer. Both the original sections were constructed on the inclined plane principle, each stage using a separate, immaculately kept steam winding en-

gine and each separated by a 'patamar' or staircase landing, on the level. These 'patamars' were worked by small oil-fired 0-4-0 tram-like engines built in the early 1900s by Kerr Stuart and Robert Stephenson, although there were some later additions in 1931. The locomotives also acted as brake engines on the inclines themselves, the engine picking up its train at Santos, then making the ascent by gripping the steel cable. At each summit the tram engine took over, moving its load to the next stage and so on up a total of five inclines. Both lines are cut into the mountainside with a succession of tunnels and viaducts over deep ravines, making the ride in the wooden passenger seats on the front of the enclosed locomotives something of an adventure.

Once the original system had been rebuilt and electrified, tried and tested, the 'new' rope-worked system was no longer needed. Fortunately, however, there has been a rescue operation using the most scenic of the inclines between the fourth and fifth 'patamars', a distance of about 1¼ miles. Four of the engines (one original Kerr Stuart, two original Robert Stephensons and one

A 5 ft 3 in gauge steam tram locomotive (No. 4 built by Kerr Stuart in 1900) stands in the smog at the bottom of the Paranapiacaba rope-worked incline near Sao Paulo in September 1977. This line is now closed to normal traffic (all services being transferred to a parallel electrified rack line) but has been reopened as a tourist attraction.

193

Two of the beautifully kept Baldwin locomotives belonging to the now preserved tourist 2 ft 6 in line running out of Sao Joao del Rei. Once an extensive narrow-gauge network, this railway still uses its old station and roundhouse; it has four operable engines and some vintage coaching stock, all kept in immaculate order. Even in happier years when the whole line was working, the locomotives were still spotless, as can be seen by the photograph of 2-8-0 No. 55 (Baldwin 10497/89) and 4-6-0 No. 38 (Baldwin 37083/11) taken at Sao Joao del Rei in September 1977.

of the later 1931 Robert Stephensons) have been kept and are used on Sunday tourist trains made up of a locomotive and two wooden coaches. The service is sometimes half-hourly, weather permitting, with easy access from the Luz station in Sao Paulo, and the journey takes about an hour. In addition, a machinery and winding house is open for display. This is heartening news, for the Santos inclines had become quite famous and it was feared that the steam operations would be gone for ever.

The second near-miracle is the preservation of a section of a truly lovely 2 ft 6 in gauge line. A couple of hundred miles north-west of Rio lies the State Railway station of Antonio Carlos. Until recent times this was joined to Sao Joao del Rei, an old colonial city with two beautiful 18th-century churches, by narrow-gauge tracks where the train of wooden coaches and some wagons was hauled by a diminutive and spotless Baldwin 2-8-0 or 4-6-0. During its working life the railway was an example of charm and efficiency; its engines were always

clean, its trains ran to time and a visit to the Sao Joao roundhouse a total joy. Services ceased in 1983 and observers feared the worst. However, the Brazilians have risen to the situation, admirably transforming a piece of real railway into a live museum. They have restored the station and rebuilt the roundhouse, and keep three Baldwin 4-4-0s, six 4-6-0s and six 2-8-0s along with several period-piece coaches. Two of the 4-6-0s and two of the 2-8-0s are in working order and in regular use. A couple of return trips are run on Fridays, Saturdays and Sundays eight miles out to Tiradentes where there is a turntable, though extra trains are often needed so popular is this fantastic operation.

The station complex including the roundhouse is open daily. The latter also contains two metre-gauge engines (one sectioned) and a Bo Bo electric. Although the hustle and bustle of trains leaving the terminus before first light is now over, the spirit of the railway remains alive, and almost as it was – a tremendous achievement by all concerned.

AUSTRALASIA

Finally, Australia and New Zealand are both countries with flourishing tourist lines rescued from oblivion by enterprising enthusiasm. The front runner has to be the 2 ft 6 in gauge Emerald Tourist Railway in Victoria, more colloquially known as the 'Puffing Billy Railway', the sole survivor of four experimental narrow-gauge lines used to develop rural areas early this century. Puffing Billy is Australia's equivalent to Great Britain's Talyllyn Railway – first in the field and second worldwide – a record to be proud of,

professionalism by the Puffing Billy Preservation Society who restored it and now operates the trains. Originally the line was worked by the Victorian Government Railways, but so important had it become that an Act of the State Parliament transferred the railway and all its assets to a newly formed authority known as the Emerald Tourist Railway Board, made up of representatives from both the Preservation Society and the Victorian government-controlled Tourist Commission. Contrary to the system in the U.S.A. where few preserved or tourist railways are volunteer-manned,

The Castlemaine and Maldon Railway is a 16-km branch running through a mixture of forest and farming land, and is run by a preservation society formed in 1976 using steam power and wooden-bodied country passenger cars. Due to protracted negotiations it was a late opener (Easter 1986) but trains now run on Sundays and most public holidays. Here, ex-Victorian Railways K class 2-8-0 No. 160 tackles the 1 in 40 grade out of Muckleford on 23 August 1987.

and it still keeps its links with the TR even though the lines are separated by half a globe. Its great advantage is that Melbourne is close at hand, with electric trains running out of Flinders Street station bringing hordes of happy Aussies bent on a good day out – which they get. The little train runs from Belgrave to Lakeside, a distance of 13 km, and the ride provides everything: beautiful Baldwin 2-6-2 tanks, trestle bridges, panoramic scenery and at the far terminus, Emerald Lake Reserve.

The Puffing Billy Railway did not just happen; it is the result of dogged determination combined with sheer

Puffing Billy makes excellent use of helpers – on similar lines to preserved railways in Great Britain.

As in the U.K. the reasons why Australian preservation and tourist lines have evolved makes an extremely varied story. For example, while the Puffing Billy operation essentially uses a former railway which was almost unique, the tourist only 3 ft 6 in gauge Zig Zag Railway about 160 kilometres west of Sydney was virtually forced to use this gauge even though it is located on the track of an ex-New South Wales 4 ft 8½ in gauge line, because almost the only motive power and stock they

With a crowded train behind the bunker, a Baldwin 2-6-2 tank makes its way across the wooden trestle *en route* from Belgrave, almost on the outskirts of Melbourne, to Emerald and Lakeside, a distance of just on 13 km. Ever popular with tourists, this 2 ft 6 in gauge railway was the first of its kind in Australia.

could get came from Queensland. This makes it historically quite out of character. Nevertheless, this particular group have excelled and have expanded their operation to a degree probably only second to Puffing Billy.

In the old days all traffic from Sydney to the west traversed the Zig Zag at Lithgow but by 1910 a ten-tunnel double-track main line was built, enabling trains to avoid this operating nuisance. It did not take long for nature to reclaim its own and the Zig Zag lay half-forgotten until 1968, when

formation to Clarence, a distance of some six kilometres.

South Australia once had two gauges – 5 ft 3 in and 3 ft 6 in – but now it has three with the transcontinental route (east-west) and the Adelaide-Alice Springs (north-south) up-graded to the standard 4 ft 8½ in gauge. The 3 ft 6 in is still there, for the Pichi Richi Railway tourist line now runs over a portion of the *original* Alice Springs Central Australian line. Although located some 300 kilometres north of Adelaide in a rather sparsely populated and

Opposite: Ex-QR class BB 18¼ Pacific No. 1072 runs tender first over one of the three stone viaducts on the Lithgow Zig Zag Railway in New South Wales. Closed and with the track taken up after the construction of a deviation line in 1910, this section of a once standard-gauge line has been reopened by a preservation organization and is now a popular tourist railway.

a group of enthusiasts took the bull by the horns and entered into negotiations for purchase; they opened the line to tourists in 1975. The Zig Zag has two tunnels, three beautiful sandstone viaducts and man-made ledges clinging to the mountainside – one of the wonders of 19th-century railway engineering. In the early days of 1987 the railway took a fascinating new step forward (helped by funding from the State government under a bi-centennial grant) and work began in the relaying of track over the old

semi-arid region, this service is also doing well attracting tourists Australia-wide, for the soil, rock and vegetation colouring is vivid, skies are pure blue and the region, generally called the Flinders Ranges, is well known as a wildflower reserve.

Another comparatively new entry on to the scene is the Hotham Valley Tourist Railway (run completely by volunteers) in Western Australia. The railway was formed in March 1974 and runs over the branch line from Pinjarra to the timber-milling town of Dwel-

Above: The Zig Zag tourist railway's new extension line in December 1987, showing an ex-Queensland Government Railway class DD17 4-6-4 tank once used on the Brisbane suburban services. The rolling stock was formally in use on the South Australian Railways.

lingup, some 24 kilometres to the east in the Darling Ranges. Steam operations began in 1976 using Manchester-built Beyer Peacock W class 4-8-2s obtained from surplus Western Australian Government Railway stock. This is an excellent tourist operation, winning the 1986 all-Australia award for Tour Services and Transportation, and two prestigious States awards in 1987 for the Best Tourist Attraction and for Tour Services and Transportation. When one adds to this a fascinating and impressive service in Tasmania known as the Van Diemen Light Railway, one finds that steam in Australia is very much alive.

In New Zealand dieselization was well under way by the mid-1950s; but main-line steam died hard and it was not until 1974 that the last small group of engines, retained for the sake of steam-heating passenger trains in the South Island, was finally withdrawn. This meant that the very active local enthusiasts had plenty of time to get organized, and in relation to the size of its population New Zealand probably

Ordered from Beyer Peacocks of Manchester and delivered in 1951–52, these 3 ft 6 in gauge W class 4-8-2s served both the Western Australian Government Railway and the Silverton Tramway. Made redundant by diesels in 1972, Nos. W933 and W934 were purchased by the Pichi Richi Railway Preservation Society in 1974 and now run over the track bed of the old narrow-gauge line to Alice Springs, Northern Territories, between Quorn and Stirling North, taking in the scenic Pichi Richi Pass. The Preservation Society provides all labour voluntarily through its members.

Two W-class 4-8-2s belonging to the Hotham Valley Tourist Railway in Western Australia take the 'Dwellingup Forest Ranger' *en route* from Pinjarra to Dwellingup. The journey involves steep grades and sharp curves as the train climbs into the Darling Ranges and Jarrah Forest on one of Australia's most scenic tourist railways.

has more active and preserved steam locomotives than any other country.

Not surprisingly, the largest concentration of this activity is close to the largest city. About 50 kilometres south of Auckland the Glenbrook Vintage Railway runs a steam service at weekends and public holidays for nine months of the year, over some eight kilometres of the ex-NZR Waiuku branch. The GVR runs through pleasant rolling country with two intermediate stations and a long 1 in 50 grade, and it has established itself as a well-supported attraction. Almost all the equipment is ex-NZR; the exception is a major one – New Zealand's only Mallet. This is a 2-4-4-2 tender engine, built by Alco in 1912 for a logging railway, and restored to service by the GVR in 1976 after 25 years of dereliction. The other engines are a Ww class 4-6-4T of 1910 and a Ja class 4-8-2 of 1946. From time to time all of them, particularly the Ja, get outings on the main line, together with some of the GVR's restored coaches.

At the Auckland Zoo are several larger NZR engines, but only a centenarian L class 2-4-0T is operational on a kilometre or so of track, alongside the last surviving Auckland tram. In the far north a steam train operation has recently been set up running on eight kilometres of almost disused NZR line on the Bay of Islands. This is a very good holiday area, but in spite of offering such attractions as a 4-8-2 steaming down the main street, the operation perhaps faces a rather precarious future. Another closed branch line, at Glen Afton in the coal-mining area some 95 kilometres south of Auckland, sees some activity with the Bush Tramway Society, who are restoring some geared locomotives once used on logging lines, as well as some small ex-colliery tank engines. At Te Awamutu, 160 kilometres south of Auckland, there is a private collection of ex-NZR locomotives, some of them now unique, but none operational. One can only hope that some of these will come to life again.

Preserved on the Glenbrook Vintage Railway, this unique locomotive once owned by the Putaruru to Mokai logging railway in the North Island was left behind when the rest of the railway was demolished and lived in a blackberry bush for many years. Built by Alco in 1912, No. 4 attacks the 1 in 50 gradient on the eight-km section of line, banked by a Ww class 4-6-4 tank of 1910.

Better things are to be found in Wellington. The Silverstreams Railway, running over a kilometre or two of track which formed the original course, before it was straightened and diverted, of the Hutt Valley suburban line, has quite a fleet of equipment, including a working Ka class 4-8-4, operated at weekends; and in the old engine shed at Paekakariki, 43 kilometres to the north, Steam Incorporated has set up an operating base for main-line steam. This was an act of faith for years, since like some other railways the NZR went through a phase of saying that steam engines would never be allowed out on main lines

again for all sorts of convincing technical reasons; meanwhile their fleet of passenger coaches was reduced to such a level that even putting extra stock on a scheduled train during peak periods was impossible, much less running even diesel-hauled specials. But in recent years this policy has been reversed – largely because of the existence of several privately owned and restored sets of coaches – and some excellent steam excursions have been run over NZR main lines. One of the first was extremely ambitious: a double-headed Ka/Ja train from Auckland to Wellington and return, 685 kilometres each way.

the *Earnslaw*. All this was in a spectacular mountain area, well filled with holidaymakers. But it was too ambitious; nowadays the NZR have leased both the steamer and the train to private operators, and the Kingston Flyer runs over a length of some 19 kilometres only, which is now over 110 kilometres from any other railway.

The two main South Island cities each have a steam railway within their boundaries. The Ocean Beach line in Dunedin operates ex-industrial locomotives on a short length of reconstructed line, while the Otago Vintage Train Trust has the largest fleet of privately owned coaches used on mainline excursion work; indeed, they have gone beyond restoration and recently completed the first new passenger coach to be built in New Zealand for 45 years. Their train has run charter trips over the whole of New Zealand, while even using diesels they have a firm home base since two sections of the NZR within 20 kilometres of Dunedin are highly spectacular and make a good half-day outing. At Ferrymead, near Christchurch, there is a re-created turn-of-the-century small town with both electric trams and a steam railway, plus a railway museum. This contains another quite large collection of ex-NZR locomotives, including another 4-8-4, mostly in running order. The Weka Pass Railway, 64 kilometres to the north, runs occasionally on eight kilometres of ex-NZR branch.

Perhaps the most incredible achievement has been at the small town of Ashburton, 80 kilometres south of Christchurch. A group set up the Plains Railway on a kilometre or so of abandoned branch line nearby, and after collecting some other vintage equipment, including an A class 0-4-0T of 1876, exhumed from some riverbank reinforcement work where it had lain buried for 50 years the ruins of an American-built K class 2-4-2 of 1878 – indeed the particular engine which had worked the first train from Christchurch to Dunedin in that year; and they have restored it to magnificent working order. This splendid machine has also been back on the main line.

Given that less than one third of the population live in the South Island, what they achieved in the way of railway preservation is perhaps even more impressive. The NZR itself led the field for a while in the 1970s and early 1980s, with an 'official' steam tourist train, the 'Kingston Flyer', running twice daily in each direction over the 61 kilometres from Lumsden to Kingston. They kept on their books for the purpose two Ab class 4-6-2s of 1916 and a dozen excellently restored coaches of the same era; while from Kingston to Queenstown they still ran a most elegant, coal-fired and reciprocating-engined lake steamer,

CHAPTER 4

NEW LIFE ON THE MAIN LINES

Preceding page: Stanier's Jubilee class 4-6-0 No. 5593 *Kolhapur* restored to its original LMS condition by the Birmingham Railway Museum blows off at Manchester Victoria station while waiting to pick up a Southport excursion in the spring of 1987.

Below: Swindon-built 1950 Castle class 4-6-0 No. 7029 *Clun Castle* hauls the first steam train for 21 years over Brunel's famous bridge across the River Tamar out of Cornwall into Devon.

GREAT BRITAIN

It is early autumn in 1985, 150 years on from the birth of Isambard Kingdom Brunel's Great Western Railway, magnificent in its Victorian splendour and its 7 ft gauge. Built to the vision of a great engineer, the tracks spread from London to Bristol, west to Exeter, then onwards crossing the river Tamar into the Royal Duchy of Cornwall, even to its westernmost tip at Penzance. But Brunel's gauge has been gone for nigh on a century, sacrificed to necessity and the universal franchise of Stephenson's wagon-wheeled 4 ft 8½ in. Steam has gone too: sleek 125 HSTs glide over the Royal Albert Bridge into Plymouth and on over computerized tracks to London's Paddington or north-east to Birmingham, York, Newcastle and even Edinburgh. Brunel's ghost may haunt Box Tunnel, where legend has it that the dawn sun shines through both portals on his birthday, while *North Star*, *Firefly*, *Lord of the Isles*, *Great Bear*, *Lode Star* and *Launceston Castle* have gone to their last rest, but it is now the age for forward-thinking railwaymen – the past is the past. There is no time or room for steam today. But every rule has its exception. Good public relations, a little nostalgia and a nose for marginal profit has brought some steam back on a controlled basis.

As the afternoon sun starts to drop down into the west and the river begins to glisten, crowds standing above the Devon bank of the Tamar look over Brunel's bridge across to the Cornish shore and hear a now strange whistle; straining their eyes they see a plume of steam drifting from a gleaming green and black steam engine over some chocolate and cream coaches. It is a picture almost forgotten; certainly one gone for well over two decades, almost a generation. The train has come east from Truro, St. Austell, Par, Lost-withiel and Liskeard; it halts at Saltash platform to allow a diesel over the single track of the bridge. Then, the puffs of white steam from its chimney visible seconds before the sound of its

exhaust carries across the water, *Clun Castle* moves the train slowly but majestically and rolls it over the spans high above the water.

Out of the last great arch it comes, the copper rim of the engine's chimney catching the sun's rays, round the curve to disappear towards Plymouth's North Road station. In the rear coach rides Sidney Newey, General Manager of British Rail's Western Region and successor to Brunel; today he has made history. Even so, it is unlikely that steam will ever become a part of the Cornish tourist scene, as the facilities for servicing are long gone, and any form of regular operation would be seen as uneconomic.

The Great Western Railway's 150th

One of the major events of 1985 was the running of double-headed steam specials over the old Great Western Railway's main line between Bristol and Plymouth. On 8 September the two preserved Castle class 4-6-0s, Nos. 7029 *Clun Castle* and 5051 *Drwsyllyn Castle*, were used with some success. The photograph shows a typical GWR/WR scene at Tiverton Junction, with sparkling green engines and Great Western semaphore signals still in use.

anniversary celebrations were a culmination of 13 years of successful steam
running over British Rail's tracks from
1972 onwards. The Great Western has
always been an evocative railway but
circumstances welded it into a shape
that created more euphoria than most.
First there was Brunel's 7 ft gauge,
either a dreadful failure or a vision
ahead of its time; the choice is a
personal one. Then there was the
railway's survival into the post-First
World War grouping; it was the only
company to remain intact – it did not
amalgamate, it accumulated. Last but
not least its efficient public relations
organization ensured Great Western
adoration in the homes of 'boys of all
ages'. No wonder that 1985 was
celebrated on high, much to the fury of
some who felt that the 'Great Way
Round' should have died in 1947 and
that all these shenanigans were not part
of a modern railway.

It was a great fling, double-headed
Castles running from Plymouth to
Bristol, a King, Castles, Halls and
Manors on the main line from Swindon to Gloucester, and above all the
return to service of the 1904 record-
breaking *City of Truro*, the first engine
to be authentically recorded at over
100 mph. But this celebration did not
just happen – to start with, apart from
its Vale of Rheidol narrow-gauge line
in Wales, British Rail does not own a
single steam locomotive.

Steam on Great Britain's main lines
died officially in the summer of 1968
and it was the authorities' intention
that it should stay dead, very dead
indeed. Back in 1951 railway preservation had begun with the revival of
the Talyllyn Railway and, as we have
seen, this and other similar railways in
Great Britain began to prosper. But
privately owned lines were one thing,
privately owned express locomotives
running over British Railways'
nationalized tracks were quite another.
The very first locomotive to be
purchased for occasional use over
British Railways' system was a small
ex-Great Northern Railway (later
LNER) 0-6-0 saddle tank; this was
owned by Captain William Smith and

Opposite: After restoration
to working order for the
1985 Great Western
Railway's 150th
anniversary celebrations,
the record-breaking 4-4-0
City of Truro has made few
forays over British
Railways' tracks. One such
occasion was on 20
December 1986 when the
engine worked two return
trips from York to
Scarborough and is seen
here on the return journey
passing Falsgrave signal
box.

Emerging into the winter sunshine from the portal of the two-mile-long Cowburn tunnel, Gresley's LNER A3 class 4-6-2 No. 4472 *Flying Scotsman* starts its run through the Hope Valley *en route* from Manchester to Spalding on 10 November 1984. The engine was working its way to Stratford (London) for the opening of the North Woolwich Museum by the Queen Mother ten days later, No. 4472 carrying her from Stratford to North Woolwich.

after running a few short excursions the engine passed on to private railways. The next locomotive to enter the scene did so with a bang; it was the famous LNER A3 class Pacific, then numbered in BR series as 60103 but more properly known as No. 4472 *Flying Scotsman*. The date of this historic purchase was 16 April 1963 and the purchaser was Alan Francis Pegler. A great deal has been written about the *Flying Scotsman* over the years and in private preservation the engine has had more than her moments, including a well-remembered but disastrous trip to America which unfortunately placed her owner in an extremely serious financial situation. But in 1963 the whole idea was an extremely novel one, especially as Pegler, who was then a member of one of British Railways' subsidiary Boards, managed to persuade the powers that were at the time to sign a running contract.

Between 1965 and 1967 (when main-line steam was all but over and most engines had been scrapped – or so everyone thought) four other express locomotives were purchased privately for active service on BR; there were two Swindon-built 4-6-0s, No. 4079 *Pendennis Castle* (M. Higson), No. 7029 *Clun Castle* (P. B. Whitehouse), LNER A4 Pacifics 4464 *Bittern* (G. Drury) and 4498 *Sir Nigel Gresley* (J. Riddick and the A4 Society). Names are deliberately mentioned here as these four people and the Society (along with Alan Pegler) were without doubt the progenitors of the main-line steam running story of today. However, the 'modern thinkers' on British Rail had the final say and in November 1967 they imposed a total ban on steam running over the Board's tracks. But they forgot Alan Pegler and his contract! So the door remained ajar.

In all there were four and a half long years when steam (except of course for the *Flying Scotsman*) was forbidden to venture over BR's lines. During that period back-door activity to restore steam to main-line service in a controlled and sensible fashion persisted and eventually this persistence was

Right: Ex-LNER A4 class 4-6-2 No. 4498 was one of the few locomotives to be purchased straight out of service and put to work on steam specials prior to the notorious steam ban from late 1967 to 1971. No. 4498, named *Sir Nigel Gresley* after her famous designer, was overhauled at Crewe Works and came into service in the autumn of 1967. The engine is seen here heading the *Shakespeare Limited* from London to Stratford upon Avon.

Opposite: One of three ex-LMS Jubilee class 4-6-0s to be preserved in working order, No. 5593 *Kolhapur* takes a special excursion out of Manchester Victoria *en route* for Southport on 14 September 1986. These locomotives were used on the London to Birmingham two-hour express trains until the early 1960s, as well as on the Midland main line.

rewarded. There were probably two main reasons for the guarded reintroduction of main-line steam running facilities. In 1968 R.L.E. Lawrence (later Sir Robert Lawrence) was Chairman and General Manager of the London Midland Region based at Euston. He was persuaded to allow steam 'open days' at the BR diesel depot at Tyseley, Birmingham, then the home of *Clun Castle* and an LMS Jubilee No. 5593 *Kolhapur*, plus Black

Five No. 5428 purchased only weeks prior to the steam ban; the agreement was on condition that BR received 50 per cent of the proceeds. Maybe Lawrence took some small risk, but it paid off as some 12,000 people turned up to the first event. Later the Tyseley 'circus' ventured out to other BR open days at London (Cricklewood) and Liverpool (Allerton). At least it was a step forward – and BR kept face by insisting engines be diesel-hauled in 'light steam' to London and Liverpool!

The second and final factor was the bulldog determination of Peter Prior, the Managing Director of the Hereford cider-making firm of Bulmer's. Prior persuaded his company to acquire a 'Cider Train' consisting of five ex-Pullman coaches, including the first-class *Aquila* built in 1951 especially for the Royal Family. This was decked out in Bulmer's livery of green, white and red. As the *pièce de résistance* Prior talked the custodians of the famous ex-GWR locomotive *King George V* into lending him the engine – including a guarantee that he would return it to working order. With all this behind him, Prior opened his 'return to steam' front and besieged all and sundry, especially (Sir) Richard Marsh, BR's new Chairman, who was more flexible and commercially minded than his predecessor, Henry Johnson. The day was won when *King George V* hauled a Bulmer's special from Hereford to a Tyseley open day on 2 October 1971;

A wet day at London's Marylebone terminus with ex-BR standard class 4 4-6-0 No. 75069 waiting with a charter train on 12 April 1986; it is almost a picture of the past with the beautiful cast-iron lamppost still proudly performing its proper task on the platform and a railway policeman in a uniform dating back to the First World War. No. 75069 is privately owned and is normally based on the Severn Valley Railway. During 1987 it was one of two engines regularly working the BR-sponsored Cambrian Coast steam specials on a regular schedule during the summer months.

nothing went wrong and everyone made money. The first 'return to steam' chartered special was run from Birmingham to Didcot behind No. 7029 *Clun Castle* in 1972 and the same year W. H. McAlpine negotiated the purchase of the beleaguered *Flying Scotsman*, paid off all the relevant debts and brought her home from America. No. 4472 arrived back at Liverpool in February 1973. The stage was set.

While all this was going on and by a quirk of fate, a near-miracle occurred in South Wales. Most of the locomotives disposed of by BR were sold to scrap merchants, who cut them up quickly and thus the majority disappeared from sight. There was one exception to the rule – the yard belonging to Woodham Brothers, Scrap Merchants and General Dealers of Barry, Glamorgan. Here over 200

locomotives sat unmolested except for the stripping of as much non-ferrous metal as Dai Woodham's workforce knew how; the bulk of the locomotive remained intact, for the brothers were using their excellent business acumen. They had disposed of the profitable brass, copper and bronze fittings – the heavy steel components such as boilers, frames, wheels and cylinders could wait. The site at Barry became unique and Woodhams soon found that there were better sales for their scrap than to the furnacemen: railway enthusiasts flocked to South Wales and most of the engines have now found homes – good, bad and indifferent – but they have been 'rescued'. The brothers may have made a fortune but the end result has been that a very large number of supposedly scrap engines have, through love, care and sheer dogged determination, been restored to running order, most on tourist lines but some to the exacting standards demanded for main-line running. In fact the majority of the tourist operations, both railways and steam centres, have purchased their locomotives from Barry.

Because of the nature of the British steam enthusiast spares have been squirrelled away, some purchased from countries such as South Africa and India. Those who have managed to raise the cash to purchase the hulks of engines (Woodhams have certainly not given these away), transport them to a decent home and actually rebuild them have given untold satisfaction and pleasure not just to themselves but to thousands of others and have produced a new tourist industry spread over the whole of the country. It is easy to be eulogistic but it is only absolute determination that has made the whole progression of today's main-line steam running possible, changing a seemingly dismal picture completely. No longer are there only five locomotives out on BR's lines, many others see regular service – and all because a small South Wales scrap merchant had other things to do than cut up his engines on arrival in his yard.

Right: One of the historic events of 1986 was the return to service of ex-LNER A4 Pacific No. 4468 *Mallard*, the holder of the world's authenticated speed record for a steam locomotive: 125 mph down Stoke bank on 4 July 1938. Belonging to and restored by the National Railway Museum, it is seen here in the classic location of York station about to leave on its first journey to Scarborough and Hull on 9 July 1986.

Preceding page top: Ex-GWR Castle class 4-6-0 No. 5080 *Defiant* being rebuilt in the Tyseley workshops of the Birmingham Railway Museum in September 1987. Rescued from Barry scrapyard, the engine has been totally stripped, firebox restayed, boiler retubed, cylinders rebored, wheel tyres returned and all fittings and pipework supplied as new. This is not unusual in today's preservation world and gives an indication of the determination and hard work necessary to restore a main-line steam locomotive to full running order.

Preceding page bottom: Proudly carrying the bell fitted during the visit to the Baltimore and Ohio Railway in 1927, Collett's GWR No. 6000 *King George V*, restored to working order in 1969 via the offices of the managing director of Bulmer's cider company, skirts the retaining wall alongside the river Severn at Purton, just north of Lydney in Gloucestershire, *en route* from Swindon to Newport and Hereford with the 'Red Dragon' on 12 October 1985.

The development of steam excursions over the nationalized system has had to be controlled; this is now formalized using a link organization known as the Steam Locomotive Operators Association, SLOA for short. BR deals only with SLOA members through a supremo in London; all steam-hauled workings have to be approved by him, as do all locomotives on the running list. But it does not end here: both privately owned locomotives and coaches have to be registered with British Rail and a fee paid for this, taking in the requisite boiler and mechanical inspections which quite properly are very strict. Boilers, for instance, require an internal examination every five years extendable under certain circumstances to seven. Locomotive owners can either charter a train for their own use (reselling the tickets and hopefully making a profit over a limited approved route) or hire the engine, either to BR who run certain steam trains themselves on a regular basis or others prepared to charter the trains through SLOA. British Rail operate a regular series of Pullman trains steam-hauled out of Marylebone terminus in London to Stratford upon Avon on Sundays, plus summer only services in the Highlands of Scotland from Fort William to Mallaig and over the Cambrian coastline in mid-Wales; other routes in regular use are Chester, Shrewsbury and Hereford to Newport, Birmingham to Didcot (Oxfordshire), Birmingham to Stratford upon Avon, York to Scarborough, and Leeds to Carlisle – over the magnificent one-time Midland railway via Settle Junction and the stark hills beyond.

In general steam locomotives operating over British Railways are based at privately owned steam depots where adequate repair and maintenance facilities are available. Most of the depots are on approved steam-running routes; these include Carnforth (Lancashire), Tyseley (Birmingham), Didcot (Oxfordshire), Bridgnorth (Severn Valley Railway) and, for those on the Sunday Pullman trains, London Marylebone. Largely due to the enterprise of enthusiasts in rescuing and restoring locomotives from Barry scrapyard (though a number *were* purchased out of service in 1968 at the eleventh hour), there is an excellent variety of types and classes available; they include LMS, LNER and Southern Railway Pacifics, a GWR King, three Castles, Halls, Manors, plus a couple of LMS Jubilee 4-6-0s and a large number of mixed traffic 4-6-0s. Add to these a supply of engines available on a non-regular basis and the resulting situation

is beyond everyone's wildest dreams in 1972.

However, although this situation is accepted today as an almost normal practice, it can never be a permanent one, depending as it does on the availability of trained steam locomotive crews from British Rail, vacuum-braked coaching stock (already in short supply) and the availability of cash not only to register and maintain the steam locomotives but also to carry out the extensive overhauls required at the conclusion of the requisite five- or seven-year periods. Although on the surface the future of main-line steam running seems more secure today than it has been in the recent past, there is a Sword of Damocles hanging over the heads of the locomotive owners unconnected with tourist railways or even steam centres – if their engines are unable to earn fees on BR's tracks to keep them alive, then the alternative strategies for survival are few indeed.

IRELAND

Across the Irish Sea, the Railway Preservation Society of Ireland has a base at Whitehead just off the Belfast to Larne line of the one-time Northern Counties Committee 5 ft 3 in gauge tracks. This is home for two sky-blue and scarlet 4-4-0s, once pride of the passenger fleet of one of Ireland's big companies, the Great Northern; they are No. 85 *Merlin*, a three-cylinder compound, and No. 171 *Slieve Gullion*, a sleekly gracious inside cylinder

simple. Whitehead is also host to a Derby-built 2-6-4 tank, two ex-Great Southern Railway 0-6-0s and some venerable coaches. Things are a little more relaxed in Ireland, with steam running out of Belfast a relatively frequent occurrence. But once a year there is a bonanza when one or more of the engines makes a trip out of the Six Counties and well down south into the Republic: it is usually a two- or three-day affair over a weekend in May.

These excursions are something to remember for the railways in Eire have a peculiar charm of their own, with long lengths of single track once west of the Dublin-Cork main line. These RPSI specials run in conjunction with the State Railways of both countries and use privately owned stock normally kept at Whitehead. The journey is always a long one, west to Sligo or Galway, south-west to Tralee or down to the south-east or perhaps to Cork where the steep gradient beginning at the platform's end makes the engine 'cough a bit'. The fare normally includes a package, taking in boxed lunches, overnight accommodation in a good hotel *and* a traditional banquet at the far terminus. Add to this a buffet bar serving draught Guinness which is open for the whole journey and the weekend is convivial to say the least; some would say that this is Irish hospitality at it best. Timekeeping is not always 100 per cent but who worries about that in such civilized surroundings? All this may sound as if the tight safety and running regulations which apply on British Rail tracks do not exist here. They most certainly do, but with less traffic about and a more gentle pace of living maybe the enjoyment is just a few points ahead.

WESTERN EUROPE

The mainland of Western Europe does not respond in quite the same way, though most countries have now relaxed their stand of 'no steam on the main lines'. Even Germany has become more easy-going than before, though it is France which makes for the winning

post with a number of big engines spread around the country. Examples of these include a 231G Pacific based just outside Rouen, then east into Lorraine a 140C 2-8-0 plus one of the real stars of the 1950s and 1960s, a 141R 2-8-2, North-American built, sturdy and always reliable; south in the Massif Central, highland country stretching south of Clermont Ferrand, there is another 141R, while a 230G (used in the film of Agatha Christie's *Murder on the Orient Express*) is shedded at Noisy-le-Sec in the eastern suburbs of Paris. And there are more.

In France, a less crowded country than Great Britain and much of it agricultural, the scale of operation differs; there are fewer locomotives in action and those which run are cared for by small cores of enthusiasts often with a railway background. The trains

219

Below: A three-coach train seen in connection with Expo Rail 83 at Nice heads through the Alpes Maritimes behind North British Locomotive Co. built 2-8-0 (ex-SNCF) No. 140C 27. The train originated at Nice and ran to Ventimiglia in Italy via Breil, returning on the coast line. This photograph was taken along the Nice-Breil section approaching Sospel on 29 March 1983.

too have a different purpose. In the U.K. these tend to run at regular intervals for the general public – for example, the Shakespeare Limited out of London on Sundays – or at irregular intervals behind special locomotives for the enthusiast market. In France trains are aimed more at the family outing, although they nearly always include a photographic run-past for those who care more deeply. Another contrast (as in Ireland) is that steam running is not limited to specific routes and although secondary lines

Right: The beautifully restored SNCF Pacific No. 231.G.558 at the end of her outward journey from Rouen to Dieppe on 14 June 1987. As on all such excursions in France, the stopover at Dieppe included facilities for an excellent meal. The restoration of No. 231.G.558 has been carried out to an extremely high standard and the locomotive is in considerable demand.

are preferred, it is far from unknown for French steam to be seen bowling along under electrified overhead wires – something normally forbidden in Great Britain. An interesting but appropriate point is that the French Ministry of Leisure and the SNCF (National Railway System) have signed an accord which gives steam respectability and enables it to operate with somewhat less formality. As has been mentioned earlier, the French also think carefully of the inner man, with good three-hour lunch stops where justice can be done to four- or five-course meals. Most of the trips are memorable, full of good humour and

fellowship, providing a pleasant day out as well as showing off a beautifully restored piece of machinery.

The Pacific Vapeur Club is one such group, based at Sotteville just outside Rouen, where they have restored one of the ex-Etat Pacifics, No. 231G558 dating from 1922 and later modified by one of steam's really great men, André Chapelon, to produce an outstanding locomotive. It made its reappearance, a culmination of six years work by Club members, on 29 June 1986 working a special train to Paris and back. As might be expected, there was a stop at Beaumont-le-Roger on the way out where Club members and friends sat down to a three-hour lunch, rising to their feet to cheer the crew to their table. The Pacific Vapeur Club also provided celebratory bottles of wine with a special label portraying their engine. The return trip from Paris to Rouen was on the main line under the wires – *Vive La France!*

Ex-SNCF class 141 TD 2-8-2 tank No. 740 at Aurillac after arrival with a private charter train from Perigueux on 20 July 1985. The French authorities tend to have a more relaxed attitude than those in either Germany or the United Kingdom (bar Northern Ireland) to the running of steam trains over their tracks, regarding such operations as an adjunct to national tourism.

NORTH AMERICA

Some of the regular steam operations in the U.S.A. are headed by Southern Pacific class GS4 No. 4449, a 4-8-4 (Lima 1941) once used to head the famous Daylight Limited between Chicago and the twin cities of Los Angeles and San Francisco. No. 4449 survived to head the Freedom Train, celebrating the bicentenary of Independence thousands of miles across the U.S.A. in 1976. Restored to the SP's magnificent livery of black, gold and red, No. 4449 crosses the Rio Grande river at El Paso, Texas (New Mexico on the right, Mexico in the background), on 14 June 1984. The train is returning to Portland, Oregon, after participating in the opening of the World's Fair in New Orleans on 14 June 1984.

Across the Atlantic Ocean in Canada and the United States, main-line steam operation has also come back, with, as mentioned earlier, the return to service of the Norfolk and Southern Corporation's 2-6-6-4 No. 1218. In fact No. 1218 is the second simple articulated engine to be restored and travel U.S. rails, its rival, Union Pacific's 4-6-6-4 Challenger No. 3985, being perhaps the better known as there was considerable publicity at the time of its comeback in 1981. The Challenger is one of the largest class of steam engines ever built, standing second only in size on the Union Pacific to the Big Boy 4-8-8-4 of the same era. The UP engine is kept at Cheyenne in Wyoming along with a modern 4-8-4 No. 8444 retained for steam specials as far back as 1960.

Unlike the railway systems of Great Britain and Western Europe, the Union Pacific still owns and maintains

these machines with a stated policy that there is 'no decision to retire them' and that 'no one wants to see them go because keeping them is like having a live dinosaur at a zoo'. But as in Europe there are problems. For example, stationed as they are in Cheyenne, the engines can service few of their supporters without travelling long distances at a prohibitive cost – and connecting railroads are not always so sympathetic to steam. Other difficulties (besides insurance) arise, as they do elsewhere, in the form of crowd control and trespass; often the rail fan is his own worst enemy. Add to this the world-wide necessity to keep costs down and to assess, quite coldly, any fringe benefits arising from publicity and public relations, and we return to the situation in the U.K. in 1972 – it all depends on an austere boardroom decision and *that* in turn usually depends on the attitude of the man at the top. A Damoclesian Sword indeed.

Above: One of the services given to the passengers on most U.S.A. main-line special trains is the 'run-past' where photographers can take full advantage of good viewpoints with the locomotive working hard. In the fall of 1969 Union Pacific's 4-8-4 No. 844 performs this service on Sherman Hill.

Left: The ultimate in narrow-gauge steam power, 2 ft 6 in gauge Rio Turbio 2-10-2 No. 119, designed by L.D. Porta, stands outside the shed at Rio Gallegos in Patagonia only a short distance from Cape Horn – the world's most southerly railway using some of its most advanced steam locomotives.

AUSTRALIA

Steam is also very much alive Down Under, where flourishing main-line tours operate most weekends in Australia. With such a huge and comparatively thinly populated land mass, distances between population centres are enormous, making it difficult to keep up with day to day matters countrywide and limiting special trains running to the more populous city areas. Sydney and Canberra (and to some extent Melbourne) are close enough together to allow participation in each other's events. Steam works extensively out of Sydney (or close thereto) with a considerable variety of motive power available; charter trains are run by the New South Wales Rail Transport Museum and one of the nearby preservation organizations, the Lachlan Valley Railway Society. These, linked with specials sponsored by the State Rail Authority of New South Wales, ensure plenty of really first-class workings. Other states have similar organizations, for example, the 5 ft 3 in gauge Victoria system has Steamrail Victoria, while the same

Former Great Western Railway Castle class 4-6-0 (sold to Australia by William McAlpine) near the inland terminus of the Hammersley Iron Railway at Paraburdoo in July 1984; there is a considerable contrast here with the work performed by this famous engine in its heyday. The line is approximately 320 km long, running from the ore mines at Paraburdoo to Dampier on the Western Australian coast.

A 60 class 4-8-4 + 4-8-4 Beyer Garratt No. 6029 heads a special tourist train near Canberra in April 1980; it was organized by the Canberra Division of the Australian Railways Historical Society. Introduced as late as 1952, the huge Garratt engines were originally intended to haul coal traffic between Lithgow and Enfield.

gauge is served in South Australia (generally out of Adelaide) by an organization going under the name of Steam Ranger. Up north it is similar, with Brisbane, Queensland's capital city, playing host to that State's branch of the Australian Railway Historical Society. Closer to home (from the British angle) the Pilbara group, way up in the remote north-west of Western Australia, even with unlimited funds had to look overseas for their steam engine, purchasing No. 4079 *Pendennis Castle* from W. H. McAlpine – good for them but a sad story for the British as 4079 is one of the more famous engines and participated in the well-known LNER/GWR locomotive exchanges of 1925.

Steamrail Victoria can be taken as a more detailed example of how main-line steam operates in Australia. This is a non-profit making organization whose aim is the retention, restoration, operation and maintenance of vintage

225

Preserved S class Baltic tank No. 3137 pilots a Baldwin-built 59 class 2-8-2 as they climb the main line on the Southern Highlands day tour from Sydney in August 1986. These 4-6-4 tanks dating from 1903–4 were built by Beyer Peacock of Manchester and proved their worth on the suburban passenger services out of Sydney. The 59XX 2-8-2s came half a century later in 1952, with the longest serving members withdrawn in 1972. Two of them, Nos. 5908 and 5910, are preserved at the New South Wales Railway Museum, Thirlmere.

locomotives and rolling stock used by the Victorian Railways (now V Line) along with other privately owned steam engines in their Steamrail's care. Most of the locomotives and rolling stock items are owned by V Line and allocated to Steamrail for restoration, maintenance and certain aspects of operation. Steamrail owns three steam and two diesel hydraulic shunting locomotives. A storage and maintenance depot is located at Newport, where most work is undertaken by volunteers who assist two full-time fitters.

Special trains are allowed to operate throughout the V Line system that is still open for passenger traffic, though trips over 'goods only' lines may be permitted from time to time if application is made. To enable a reasonable variety of destinations to be offered, Steamrail has, since 1965, paid V Line to service and maintain many turn-

tables and watering facilities; although the State Railway also makes use of these facilities for their own operational requirements, no reduction in the retention price is given to Steamrail.

Other concessions have also been obtained – for example, through co-operation with the Loco Engineman's Union, tender first operation of steam locos is permitted on lines for a distance of 40 kilometres beyond turning points, and in special circumstances this distance may be extended (centennial celebrations, etc.). Locomotives are crewed by V Line staff, while Steamrail is responsible for coaling and watering during the journey – all very much like main-line operations in Great Britain. Once V Line charges and vital insurance costs have been met, any profit from special train operators is directed to restoration of rolling stock.

Right: New Zealand never possessed pure express passenger engines but the Ka class 4-8-4s, first built in 1939, worked major services, both passenger and freight. Two have been preserved, Nos. 945 and 950, both of which are resident in the North Island. This photograph shows No. 945 at Taihape in 1966 on a special excursion working.

Opposite: R Class 4-6-4 No. R707 was one of 70 built by the North British Locomotive Company, Glasgow, in 1951 for Victorian Railways. (It was the Company's 27,000th steam engine.) Handicapped from the start by a simultaneous delivery of diesels, R707 did not enter operations until 1954 and was used on revenue services for 20 years, albeit running only 200,000 km and spending half its time out of use. In 1980 two Victorian Railways' drivers put together a team to restore the engine to a high professional standard and after six years of hard work R707 went back into the running of main-line trains.

On the first Sunday of every month Steamrail runs 'The Vintage Train' to destinations of tourist interest. Generally the motive power is steam, but in the dry Australian summers when fire bans may be in force, diesel locomotives are substituted. Other trips are operated on a charter basis for various organizations, including rail enthusiast groups, where locomotives and/or carriages are hired out for special trains. Some 30 carriages are allocated to Steamrail, with 20 of these available for operations while the remainder are under restoration.

So Australia has done well with main-line running, the various state systems co-operating with tour operators and locomotive owners. There is a great variety of power available too, from 19th-century Beyer Peacock 4-6-0s to huge 4-8-4 + 4-8-4 Garratts. In 1988 Australia celebrated her bicentenary and marked it by no less than nine inter-capital steam rail tours using a 1940s vintage train over the 4 ft 8½ in gauge lines from Perth to Adelaide, Broken Hill, Sydney, Melbourne and Brisbane; the motive power was a green, streamlined 38 class Pacific. All this was agreed and sponsored by an association of the five government-owned rail system. It shows just what *can* be done if there is a will.

TOMORROW'S STEAM

As far as most of the world is concerned, the steam locomotive is a thing of the past. There are ever increasing tourist and museum-type operations in Europe and the U.S.A. but these are minuscule compared with day-to-day traffic, and although in parts of the Third World and in developing countries such as India or China steam is still in everyday use, the question is – how long will it last and does it have any real tomorrow?

Although rated as inefficient compared with the diesel, the steam locomotive was not necessarily the dirty machine depicted in photographs of run-down sheds with coal dust and ash everywhere; good organization or the successful use of oil as a fuel could see to that. Even so, once the overall capital costs of dieselization or electrification had been met, there was no real contest.

To the operators the new forms of motive power were far less labour-intensive and had a much higher availability ratio; if one was going to use oil as a fuel, better to do so with a more effective machine albeit a more complicated one. So railway by railway, country by country, they trained new engineers, new footplate staff, new administrators, and moved into 'modern thinking'. At the same time 'aid' in the form of diesel locomotives was poured into ex-colonial countries, as well as those regarded as possible bastions against the spread of communism. It was forgotten that the steam engine was a simple machine, which usually went on working even when it felt ill and that spare parts were easy enough to manufacture or even to improvise.

At first the diesels were greeted with open arms: all you had to do was press a button and off you went. But once heavy maintenance became due, the problems started: technical skills were few, spare parts expensive and hard to come by from overseas and those were often complicated in themselves. The diesel electric locomotive in particular is a complex machine. So steam, stuck away in sidings, sometimes had to come to the rescue, which was fine for

as long as there were spares available or enough locomotives left to cannibalize. After that, what then?

In steam's Indian summer the engineers had done their best to make running and maintenance more efficient. André Chapelon in France concentrated on internal steam flows and thermodynamics, while others came forward with ideas such as multiple blast pipes and double chimneys; this improved the situation considerably but it all came late – too late. One last-ditch stand in Europe was made by Dr Adolph Giesl-Gieslingen who invented a multiple orifice blast pipe with a flat chimney of ugly but distinctive appearance, which he sold in large quantities to the Austrian State Railways and even to East Africa. He came to Britain at the eleventh hour and fifty-ninth minute and persuaded those in authority to modify a Battle of Britain class Pacific and a 9F 2-10-0; the engines were tested, though nothing else happened. Was Giesl given a fair hearing?

In a letter to the doctor dated as late as 16 October 1962, R. G. Jarvis, the technical assistant at Brighton Works responsible for the conversion and testing of the West Country Pacific, wrote that the engine concerned was performing excellently 'such that now we have a locomotive with a steaming capacity in excess of that obtained hitherto with this class, spark emission is eliminated and exhaust steam and gases no longer blowing down over the cab windows'. He added that 'consideration is now being given to the question of providing this equipment on the other 49 locomotives of the class'. But it was not to be and No. 34061 was the only engine to be Gieselized. Like the valiant work done in the U.S.A. on the Norfolk & Western class J 4-8-4, improvements came too late; it was impossible in a developed country to hold out against the advantages of diesel or electric power.

Meanwhile, in less fortunate areas of the world, others were using new knowledge to some advantage. L. D. Porta, an Argentine locomotive engineer, built on Chapelon's experience

Left top: Class 19D 4-8-2 No. 2644 was rebuilt at Beaconsfield running shed in 1979 to incorporate a Gas Producer Combustion System, Lempor double-exhaust and a few other minor improvements. Most of the new components were made at various mechanical workshops but the fitting was performed at a running shed to minimize cost; this imposed a limit on the extent of the modifications. Reclassified 19DW, the locomotive was christened *Irene*, after the designer's wife, by the shed staff at the locomotive's base at Mafeking. No. 2644 is seen here on the 06.58 Mafeking to Kimberley passenger train on 13 September 1982.

Left bottom: Class 25NC 4-8-4 No. 3450 was reconstructed at Salt River workshops on a more extensive scale, emerging in 1981. The lessons learned from 2644 were incorporated but many additional features were included to further enhance the efficiency and reduce maintenance. The resulting locomotive was so far removed from the original as to be reclassified 26. The official plates bear the name 'L.D. Porta' but she was nicknamed *Red Devil*, a name that caught the public imagination and effectively precluded any change to a more sober colour scheme. The engine is shown attached to saloon Z14130 at Beaconsfield shed, preparing for a trip to Bloemfontein on 8 September 1982.

Right: Two newly painted QJ 2-10-2s outside the works at China's Datong steam locomotive factory. On the right in red oxide undercoat is another QJ undergoing steam tests prior to painting. To the left, out of sight, is the huge works conglomeration comprising the factory itself, casting shops, machine shops and wheel shops, and accommodation for the total workforce of thousands. This remote factory is almost on the border of Inner Mongolia, where the countryside is stark in winter and relatively lush in summer.

and considerably improved a number of machines in his care, including work on boiler design, lubrication and exhaust systems. He also invented a new method for coal firing, known as the Gas Producer Combustion System, which can dramatically increase the steam engine's efficiency. As has been mentioned earlier, all this was put into use in wildest Patagonia on the 760 mm gauge line carrying coal from the mines at Turbio to the Port of Rio Gallegos some 155 miles distant. The engines are modern ones, Japanese-built 2-10-2s, 48 tonne machines delivered between 1956 and 1964. Rebuilt by Porta they are superb examples of steam motive power, regularly hauling 1,700-tonne trains while working over some of the most inhospitable countryside in the world.

Again in the southern hemisphere. David Wardale, Assistant Mechanical Engineer (Steam) to South Africa Railways, redesigned and rebuilt examples of two classes of steam locomotives incorporating Porta's ideas plus some of his own. The first engine so treated was a 19D class 4-8-2 (this particular choice was a black sheep locomotive) and a class 25NC 4-8-4. The 19D rebuild incorporated the Gas Producer Combustion System along with a double Lempor exhaust and Eastern European-type smoke deflectors, giving a saving of between 15 and 25 per cent in coal compared to similar engines of the class. The modern and efficient class 25NC fared even better. The locomotive picked, No. 3450, was rebuilt in 1981, taking in all the improvements at Wardale's disposal, and as mentioned earlier, it was painted red and aptly nicknamed *Red Devil* – the 19D had been called *Irene* after David Wardale's wife. The result? Coal consumption was cut by 28 per cent and water by 30 per cent with the maximum power output up by 43 per cent to over 4,000 abhp.

By any standards these results were outstanding, making steam and diesel performance comparable, and they are a striking example of how modern technology can be applied to the steam locomotive if the will is there to do it.

Unfortunately the railway authorities appear to feel that steam has no place in a 'forward looking' pattern so, like the earlier improvements, Wardale's work has come too late; maybe complacency in earlier years is much to blame. But the decision seems a strange one in a country which has no oil of its own, and is beleaguered in its supplies; even

with its internal problems South Africa has an abundant supply of inexpensive labour coupled with first-class mining facilities.

David Wardale is still hard at work seeking to improve steam performance, this time in a country where the political climate may prove to be better – the Peoples Republic of China. He is currently working at Datong on a project to modify and improve the design of the already modern and efficient QJ 2-10-2. So far two variants of the Gas Producer System have been tried but no prototype is yet running in service. Only time will tell if the effects of this experimentation are to bear fruit or not: politics with a small p will

while Phil Girdlestone was Works Superintendent at Boston Lodge. *Linda* did everything that was expected of her after conversion; availability (a vital point in turn-rounds on a short-haul railway), abolition of fire risk, and an economy of some 30 per cent in the then costs of oil firing. But events can rebound on themselves and with the price of oil now at a lower level, this fuel has come back into use, though the other improvements to *Linda* including the Lempor exhaust system still show considerable benefit.

Like David Wardale, Phil Girdlestone left his first love and moved on to the developing world through his work with Hugh Phillips. The rebuilding of the Sudanese engines has produced a fuel economy of 12 per cent, with the Lempor exhaust successfully tested straight from the drawing-board – something of an achievement. Moreover, the steam engines were rehabilitated at half the cost of diesels

Above: One of the 310 class 2-8-2 locomotives, No. 312 in steam outside Sennar Junction shed during a visit by the staff of Hugh Phillips Engineering Limited of South Wales. Steam officially finished on Sudan Railways in the late 1970s but one or two small pockets still survived at Kosti and Sennar.

Right: The ex-Penrhyn Quarry 0-4-0 tender tank *Linda*, modified to incorporate the gas Producer Combustion System and Lempor exhaust by Phil Girdlestone and the team at Boston Lodge Works, comes over the spiral on the new deviation line above Dduallt station on the Festiniog Railway with the 13.10 from Porthmadog to Blaenau Festiniog on 24 August 1985.

almost certainly decide the matter. But at least there is still a question mark and maybe – very much a maybe – there could be some steam in China tomorrow. If so, the effect will be profound for there are almost 5,000 QJs at work and more being built every month. All one can say is that the Chinese never sleep.

Closer to home, mention has already been made of Porta's principles being adopted by Phil Girdlestone both when working for the Festiniog Railway in North Wales and later when with Hugh Phillips Engineering in the rebuilding and resuscitation of steam engines in the Sudan. In the early 1970s the Festiniog Railway was under severe pressure from the Forestry Commission over fire risk, which led to the conversion of its fleet of locomotives to oil firing. Almost a decade later with oil prices rising steadily (making even the waste oil used for locomotive firing expensive), thought was given to redesigning *Linda*, one of the ex-Penrhyn Railway 0-4-0 tender tanks, to incorporate the Gas Producer Combustion System, Lempor exhaust and other improvements; this was all done

dealt with at the same time. But there is no knowing how far this accepted aid for steam resuscitation is a political ploy. Certainly in early 1988 reconstituted steam was still running but if the diesels work, then it is they not the steam locomotive which are preferred.

During the late 1950s the word went out that steam locomotives were outdated, labour-intensive and inefficient. Maybe they are in a Western world where wages and salaries are high and money can sometimes equate with God, but in the so-called developing countries (that is most of the world), a new look at the future could well be advisable; certainly Zimbabwe, the Sudan, South Africa and Argentina have lit more than candles to light the way. Sadly politics of any kind intrude into each and every railway's development. Chapelon, Porta, Wardale and Girdlestone have shown what is possible but there is a very big question mark as to whether there really will be steam tomorrow, for Datong is scheduled to cease new construction at the end of 1988. Existing steam may be modified and improved, but for how long is anyone's guess.

Because of the severe effects of famine, a large amount of international aid was given to Sudan in 1985–86. To enable famine relief traffic to roll in the south-west of the country, six 310 class 2-8-2 locomotives (suitable because of their light axle loading) were overhauled using E.E.C.-funded aid. The work was carried out jointly by the Sudan Railways Corporation and Hugh Phillips Engineering Limited. The first locomotive to be completed under this scheme was No. 313, seen here shunting at Atbara works yard after returning from a successful testing of the new Lempor exhaust system.

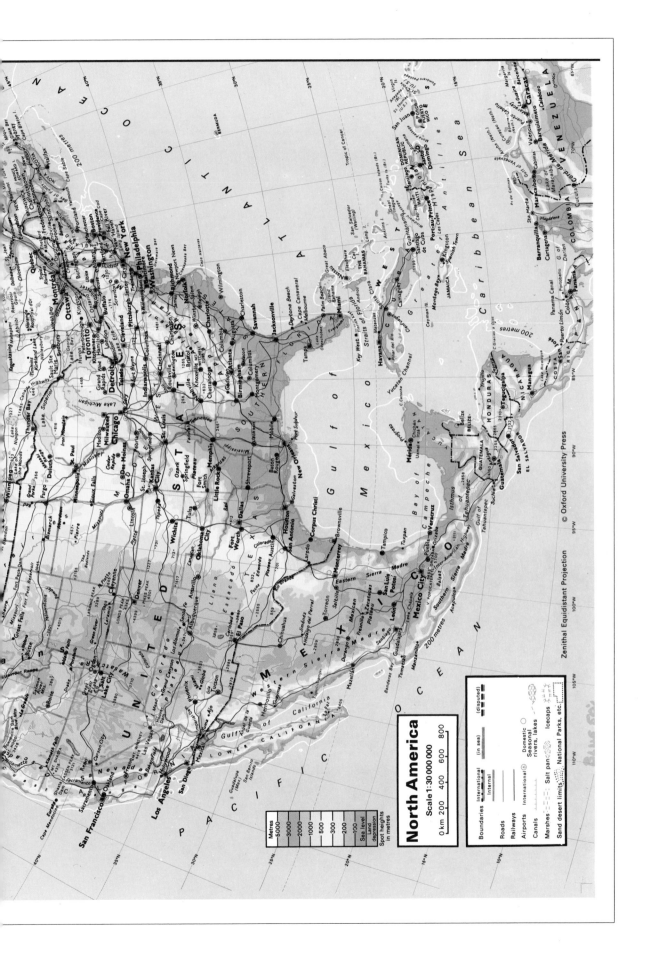

North America

Scale 1:30 000 000

0 km 200 400 600 800

Metres
5000
3000
2000
1000
500
300
200
100
Sea level
Land depression
Spot heights in metres

Boundaries International
Internal
(in sea)
(disputed)
Roads
Railways
Airports International
Domestic
Canals
Seasonal rivers, lakes
Icecaps
Marshes
Salt pan
National Parks, etc.
Sand desert limits

© Oxford University Press

Zenithal Equidistant Projection

South America

Scale 1:35 000 000

0 km 200 400 600 800

Boundaries	International	(in sea)	(disputed)
	Internal		
Roads	Motorways	Other roads	Tracks
Railways			
Airports	International ⊕	Domestic ⊕	
Canals		Seasonal rivers, lakes ○	
Marshes		Salt pan	Icecaps
Sand desert limits		National Parks, etc.	

Transverse Mercator Projection
© Oxford University Press

Metres
5000
3000
2000
1000
500
300
200
100
Sea level
Land depression

Spot heights in metres

Australasia

Scale 1:27 000 000

0   350   700 km

© Oxford University Press

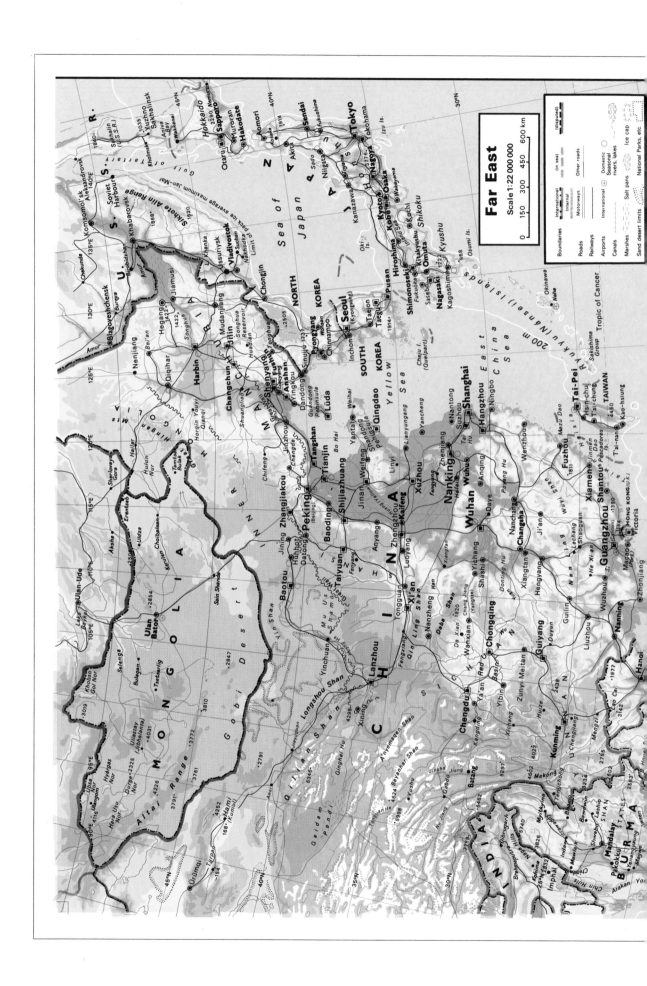

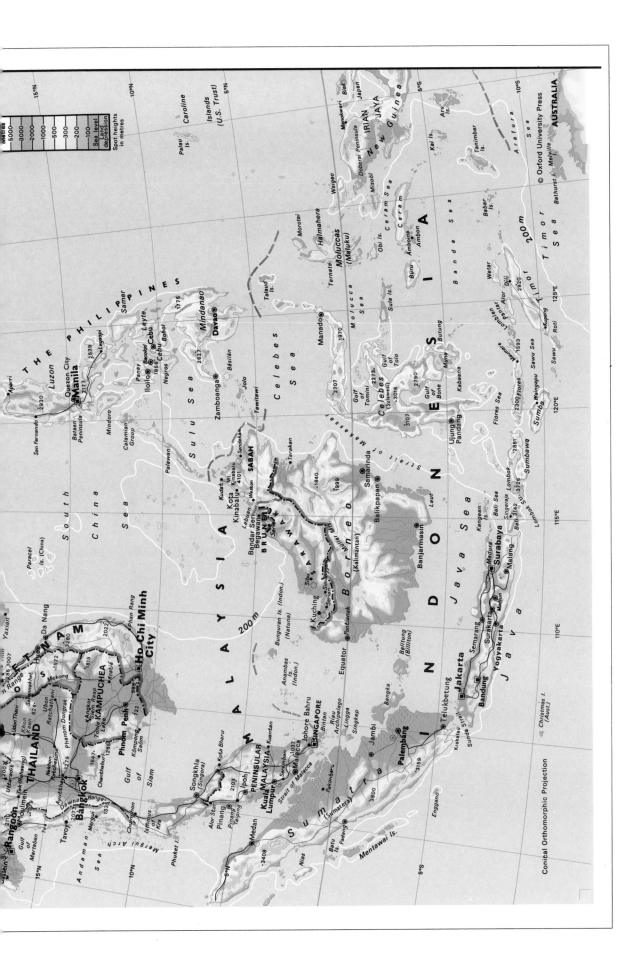

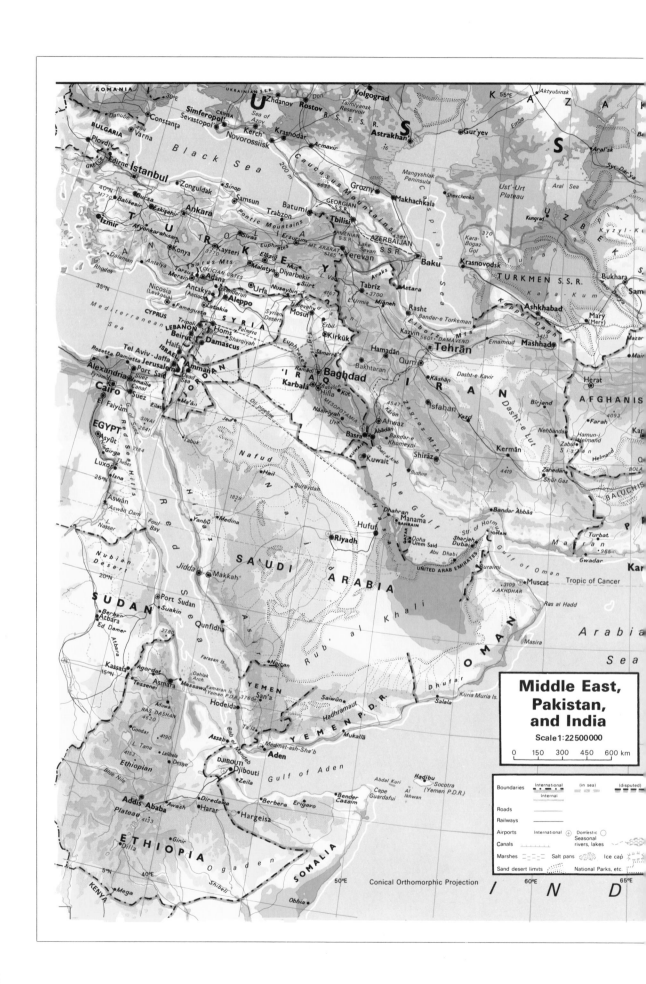

Middle East, Pakistan, and India

Scale 1:22 500 000

0   150   300   450   600 km

Boundaries	International	(in sea)	(disputed)
	Internal		
Roads			
Railways			
Airports	International	Domestic	
Canals		Seasonal rivers, lakes	
Marshes	Salt pans	Ice cap	
Sand desert limits	National Parks, etc.		

Conical Orthomorphic Projection

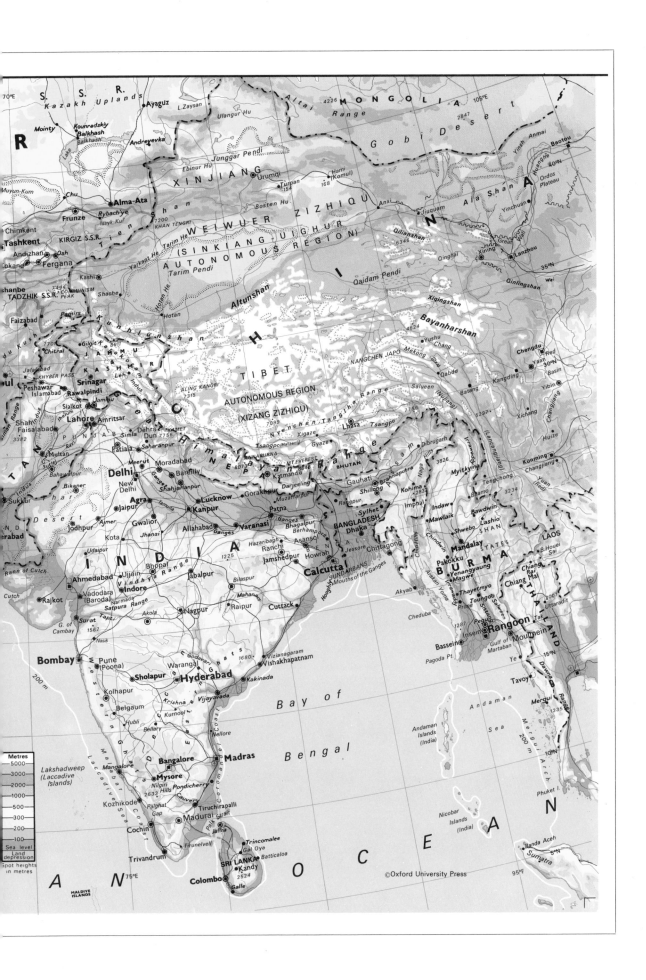

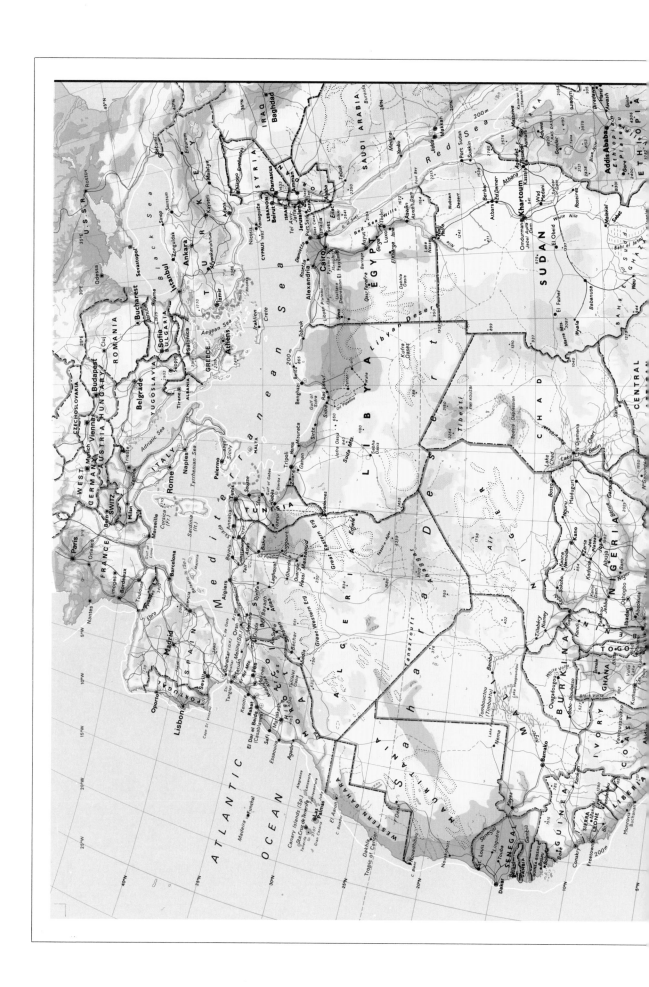

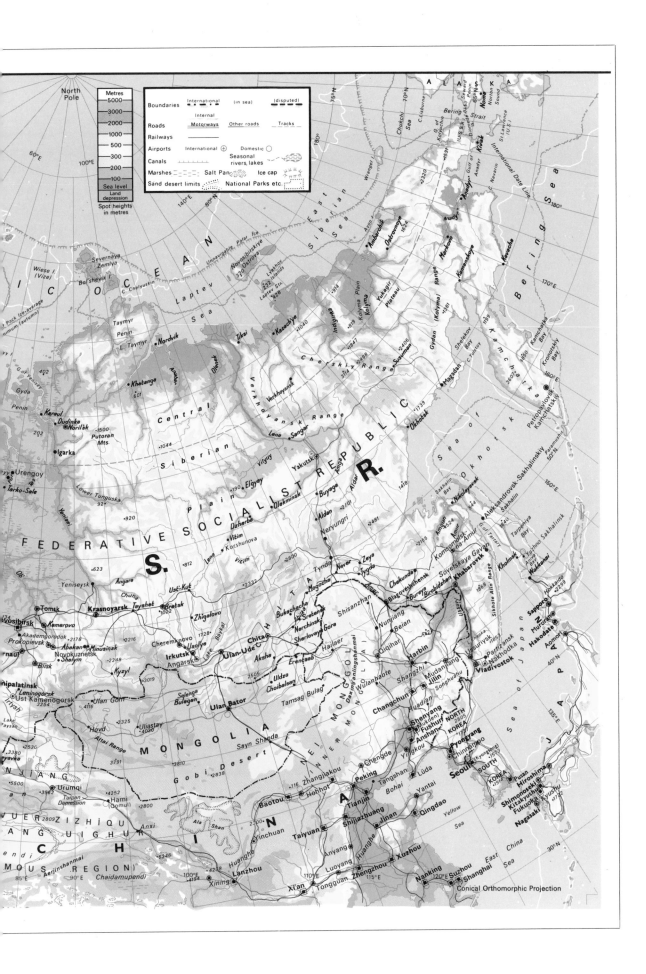

INDEX

252

253

BIBLIOGRAPHY

On The Narrow Gauge, P. B. Whitehouse (Thomas Nelson, 1964)

Narrow Gauge Railways of Europe, P. C. Allen and P. B. Whitehouse (Ian Allen, 1959)

Lines of Character, L. T. C. Rolt and P. B. Whitehouse (Constable, 1952)

Festiniog Railway Revival, P. B. Whitehouse (Ian Allan, 1963)

Steam Passenger Locomotives, J. B. Hollingsworth (Salamander, 1982)

The Last Parade, P. B. Whitehouse (New Cavendish Books, 1976)

Steam Passenger Service Directory, Empire State Railway Museum (1986)

PNKA Power Parade, Indonesian Steam Locomotives, A. E. Durrant (Continental Railway Circle)

Great Little Railways, (BBC, 1984)

Steam In Africa, A. E. Durrant, C. P. Lewis and A. A. Jorgensen (Hamlyn, 1981)

Periodicals: *Steam Railway, Railway World, Railway Magazine, Trains Magazine, Continental Railway Journal, TEFS* magazines, *Railway Gazette International*